Color Tab Index

Start Here by Learning Yellow-rumped Warblers

Warblers with Yellow

Extensive yellow on body

Yellow limited to throat and upper breast

Small patches of yellow

Warblers with Any Obvious Orange, Red, or Chestnut

Warblers with No Yellow, Orange, Red, or Chestnut

Black-and-white-striped

Blue or turquoise above

Brown above, boldly streaked below

Drab with few markings

Dull fall warblers (immatures)

STOKES FIELD GUIDE TO WARBLERS

Donald and Lillian Stokes

Maps by Thomas Young

Little, Brown and Company

Boston　New York　London

First Edition

Library of Congress Cataloging-in-Publication Data
Stokes, Donald W.
    Stokes field guide to warblers / by Donald and Lillian Stokes ; maps by Thomas
  Young. — 1st ed.
      p.   cm.
    ISBN 0-316-81664-7 (pb)
    1. Wood warblers.   2. Wood warblers — North America.   I. Stokes, Lillian Q.
II. Title.

QL696.P2438S74 2004
598.8'72 — dc22   2003053241

10   9   8   7   6   5   4   3   2   1

Imago

Printed in Hong Kong

Contents

How to Use This Guide

Stokes Field Guide to Warblers is designed to help you learn how to identify warblers. It is much more than just a collection of field clues; it is a teaching aid that will lead you to being more confident in your identification skills. Identifying warblers can seem challenging, but with this guide you will be able to more quickly narrow down the choices and come up with a name for the bird you have seen. Here is a description of the various helpful features of this guide.

Color Tab Index

The Color Tab Index on the first and last pages of the book is your entryway into warbler identification. The very first tab leads you to the chapter "Start Here by Learning Yellow-rumped Warblers." The information in this chapter will help you become familiar with the most commonly seen warbler in migration. You can skip this tab if you like and go right to the identification accounts, but sometime when you are at home, take a few minutes to look over this section.

The next tabs can be used in the field as you look at the birds. Once you see a warbler, look for the extent and placement of bright colors. If there is any yellow on the warbler, then look through the "Warblers with Yellow" tabs. If there is extensive yellow on the underparts and sometimes the whole body, choose the "Extensive yellow on body" tab. This is the largest group of warblers, and the birds are organized within this group roughly according to how much yellow they have, the ones with the most extensive yellow coming first.

If the yellow is limited to the throat and upper breast, then choose that tab. If there are only small patches of yellow on the head, throat, or sides of the breast, then choose the "Small patches of yellow" tab.

If there is any obvious orange, red, or chestnut on the warbler, choose the corresponding tab.

If the warbler has no yellow, orange, red, or chestnut, then choose among the last five tabs. The black-and-white-striped warblers are obvious, and there are three species. There are only two species that fit the "Blue or turquoise above" tab. And three warblers fit the "Brown above, boldly streaked below" tab.

The last two tabs in this section lead to the warblers with the fewest distinctive characteristics. They are presented in two groups to help you narrow down the choices. In spring, you need not check the "Dull fall warblers" tab, for these plumages are seen only in fall. In fall, you need to check both tabs when you see a dull or drab warbler.

Many birders typically find the dull fall warblers the hardest group to identify, so we have included extra pages of text in this color tab section to help you sort out these immature birds.

Species Descriptions

Each of the 51 species of warblers regularly seen in the United States and Canada has a full identification description. In this, the common name of the bird is listed first, followed by the scientific name and the bird's length. Length is a measurement of the bird from the tip of the tail to the tip of the bill.

Visual clues to identification are divided into **Main Year-round Clues** and then **Additional Clues,** organized by sex, age, or season. Main Year-round Clues are those that apply to the bird regardless of season; these are often the best and most essential clues for identification. Additional Clues point out any obvious plumage variation due to season or the sex or age of the bird. When there are no Additional Clues, it means that everything you can see about that warbler is already covered in the Main Year-round Clues.

Three warblers — Palm, Orange-crowned, and Yellow-rumped — have marked geographic differences in appearance, making it necessary to include them under two different color tabs. For each of these species, we include two full species descriptions.

Several other warblers have marked seasonal, age-related, or sexual differences in appearance and are also pictured under two or more color tabs. For these plumages we have created abbreviated accounts that include only a photograph, I.D. clues, and a page reference to the full species description.

Voice

Warbler songs and calls can be extremely helpful when you are trying to locate and identify the birds. Descriptions of songs are given, sometimes with a word equivalent that will help you to remember it. In most cases, calls are not described, because their written descriptions are inadequate no matter what you do — they all start being described as "tsit," "tsip," "tset," et cetera. In some cases, when the call of a species is very distinctive and a helpful clue for beginners, it is included.

The best way to learn the songs and calls of warblers is to listen to *Stokes Field Guide to Bird Songs, Eastern Region* or *Western Region.* To help you reference this, we have listed the CD number and track number of each species' songs and calls at the end of the Voice section. For example, *East: Disk 1, track 25.*

Behavior and Habitat

Behavior refers to a movement or action of a species that is distinctive and will help you identify it. Habitat includes a description of where the bird tends to feed and the vegetative characteristics of where it breeds.

Range and Migration Maps

The range and migration maps are special innovations of this guide. We have included them because many of our warblers breed in the far north and winter in Central and South America. Thus our best time to see them is during migration. The traditional range map does not show when and where a bird can be seen during migration; these maps do.

Key to the Maps

Each species description includes two maps with these features:

♦ The yellow-shaded area shows the summer, or breeding, range.
♦ The blue-shaded area shows the winter, or nonbreeding, range.

♦ The green area shows the year-round range, where a species breeds and spends the winter.
♦ The dotted red lines and the dates beside them show where and when a species occurs during migration. (See below for more information on how to interpret these lines.)
♦ The spring migration map shows the routes and timing of a species as the bird flies north; the fall migration map shows the routes and timing of a species as it flies south.

Below each map, there is also a sentence or two providing more information about the migration of the species. This information may be on any of several topics, such as migration routes, abundance during migration, size of the flocks in which the species is typically seen, timing of migration, habitats used during migration, or when and where the species is seen outside its migration path.

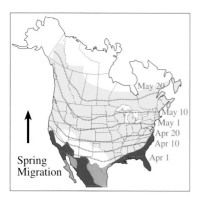

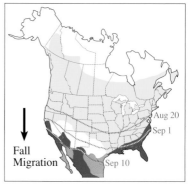

Additional Information on the Dotted Red Lines

Migration route — The dotted red lines are drawn across the entire width of a species' regular migration route. If a map has long lines drawn from coast to coast, then this species can be seen all across the country. Shorter lines indicate a narrower migration route and a more limited area in which the bird can commonly be seen. For some species, fall and spring migration routes are different.

Warblers can wander slightly during migration, so individuals may be seen outside a species' regular migration route.

Timing of the first major wave of migrants — The date that appears by each red line tells when the first major wave of migrants of a species arrives in that area. These dates are averages based on many years of field observation by hundreds of observers. Individuals and small flocks may arrive earlier and other waves may occur later.

The dates are presented in 10-day intervals, because warbler migration can occur quickly and we wanted to show enough detail to enable you to time the migration accurately and not miss seeing warblers in your area.

Several weather-related factors may alter the timing of migration. For example, a storm front may cause birds to delay their departure. Also, a warm front may trigger early northward movement, while a cold front may trigger early southward movement. Tailwinds may push birds farther than they intend to go, while headwinds hinder migration. Lateral winds can cause birds to drift off course. Very strong winds, regardless of direction, can temporarily stop birds (especially smaller birds) from migrating. A steady rain can bring migration to a temporary halt. Fog has the same effect.

Depending on which of these factors come into play, you may notice the first major wave of a species in your area arriving either before or after the date shown on the maps.

Photographs and Drawings

Photographs have been carefully chosen to represent the most important plumages that the average observer is likely to see. Every warbler species has a variety of plumages and conditions of plumage, and it would be impossible to include them all in any guide. And remember that each individual warbler can look slightly different from others of its species; whether you are using a drawn picture or a photograph for identification, it is only a representation of one bird. In every case we have tried to select photographs that best represent a species.

For each species we have also included a diagram of the shape and patterns of colors on the undertail and undertail coverts. The undertail coverts are the group of feathers that cover the base of the tail. These patterns and colors can be very useful in some identifications. This is partly because warblers are often above us in the trees and this is what you may see best. Another reason is that you may be able to eliminate a species from contention by the colors and patterns you see there. These drawings are only an approximation of the main features and are not meant to be detailed representations.

Warbler Conservation Status

Following the Identification Pages are individual accounts of the conservation status of the warblers included in this guide. These accounts focus on population trends and factors such as habitat loss and weather conditions that may influence these trends. It is our hope that this information will enhance your awareness of the habitat needs and status of the birds around you and will encourage you to participate in actively protecting the natural world.

What Is a Warbler?

The warblers of North America are often referred to as Wood-warblers, and except for one species, they are in the family Parulidae. They all have 9 outer wing feathers (primaries), 9 inner wing feathers (secondaries), and 12 tail feathers (rectrices). The exception is the Olive Warbler, which is in its own family, Peucedramidae, and has 10 primaries instead of 9. But none of this will help you know what a warbler is when you see it.

How will you know a warbler when you see it? Here are the characteristics shared by most warblers. They should help you distinguish warblers from most other birds.

Color and Pattern

Most warblers are colorful. Yellow is very common on warblers, especially underneath; green and gray often occur on the back; black streaks on the back or flanks are common, as are black facial patterns; white is found on the wingbars or as a background color underneath. Occasionally you will see chestnut, orange, or red. The patterns on the faces of many warblers are complex.

Size and Shape

Almost all warblers are small, ranging from 4¼ to 5½ inches long — about the size of a chickadee (the exception is the larger

Yellow-breasted Chat). They are streamlined in shape, with relatively small heads and slim bodies that taper to the rear. Their bills are fine, pointed, and short, designed for the most part to pick caterpillars off leaves and catch other insects. Their tails vary in length from short to average.

Behavior

Behavior can also be a good clue. Most warblers are very quick and agile as they forage, flitting about from spot to spot within a leafy canopy. They are often faster and more active than even the chickadees which they frequently accompany. It can be difficult to get a good long look at any warbler; usually you just get a few seconds at a time. Many warblers glean insects off leaves and therefore spend time searching within leaf clusters at the tips of branches. In spring and fall migration they are usually in small flocks of several species, sometimes following resident flocks of chickadees and titmice as they forage.

Songs

Warbler songs are given from early spring into summer. Most species sing less once they attract a mate. Some species start singing during spring migration and are more likely to sing the closer they get to their breeding grounds. Hearing their songs can be a good way to locate warblers during spring migration. In general, only the males sing, and on the breeding grounds, they usually do so from a medium-high to high exposed perch, offering you one of the best chances to get a good look at a warbler.

Most warbler songs are very high-pitched. Some are a series of high whistled notes on the same or different pitches; others are high-pitched trills. None are long or particularly melodic. In general, the highest-pitched songs are from warblers that live high in trees, such as Blackburnian and Cape May Warblers, while the lowest-pitched songs are from warblers that live mostly on or near the ground, like the waterthrushes and the Kentucky Warbler.

Species You May Confuse with Warblers

Several other groups of birds are often confused with warblers, particularly kinglets, vireos, and gnatcatchers.

Ruby-crowned Kinglet

Kinglets

The kinglets — Ruby-crowned and Golden-crowned — are small birds and often seen with migrating flocks of warblers. Kinglets are even smaller than most warblers and have the habit of continually flicking their wings as they feed. Some warblers may do this but not to such an extent.

Red-eyed Vireo

Vireos

Some vireos have coloring similar to that of warblers, with yellow underneath and green above. They also feed in tree canopies, gleaning insects off leaves, and may be seen with warblers during migration. They differ in having thicker bills and in their movements, which are typically slower and more deliberate as they forage. They overlap in size with warblers.

Blue-gray Gnatcatcher

Gnatcatchers

Gnatcatchers are smaller than most warblers, have very long tails, which are often flipped about, and are mostly gray above and whitish below. They also can be seen with migrating warblers.

How to Identify Warblers

Warblers are among the most beautiful birds in North America because they are so brightly colored. They are like little jewels in the treetops, tantalizing you with brief glimpses. Once you see one, you inevitably will want to see more. For some people, watching warblers during spring and fall migration is almost an obsession — a wonderful obsession.

Some people find that although they love to look at warblers, they have trouble identifying them. There seem to be an endless number of species and plumages. But this is actually not the case at all. And this field guide is designed to help make the process of identifying warblers simple and fun. "Start Here by Learning Yellow-rumped Warblers," pages 33–39, will give you help with this ubiquitous warbler, and the Color Tab Index on the first page of this book will help you narrow down the choices as you make your identification.

How Many Warblers?

There are 51 species of warblers that can be seen in North America north of Mexico. It is a wonderful challenge to find as many species as you can. In any given area, you are very likely to see about 10 species that are common. This will just whet your appetite, and you will want to spend more mornings outside during spring and fall migration. If you continue to look throughout the migration periods, you can see early, middle, and late migrating species and add another 10–20 species, depending on where you live. For even more, you can increase your fun by traveling to different habitats or geographic regions, or go to an exceptional migration "hotspot" for warblers (see page 26).

Equipment for Watching Warblers

To watch warblers you need a good pair of binoculars, and you will need to practice getting them quickly onto a bird and then trying to follow its movements. To spot a bird through your binoculars, first locate it with the naked eye. Keep your gaze fixed on the bird and raise your binoculars to your eyes. As much as possible, have the focus preadjusted to the trees where the warblers are; this will save valuable seconds as you watch the bird. Full-sized binoculars with a magnification power of about 7–8 times and a wide field of view are best for warbler-watching. Get full-sized binoculars, not small versions, as they will have a small field of view and make it harder to spot these beautiful birds. There are definitely some binocular skills that need to be developed to get good views of warblers.

Bring along this guide or our *Stokes Field Guide to Birds.* In spring, a recording of the sounds of warblers is also very helpful. See our *Stokes Field Guide to Bird Songs, Eastern Region* or *Western Region*. It is available as cassettes or compact disks that can be played in the car after you look at the warblers and hear a song. The CD disk number and track number are listed for each species in the Voice section of the species description. Many people also start to play warbler songs in their cars as they drive around in spring, just before migration starts, to refresh their memory of some of the basic songs and calls.

A telescope is almost never needed while looking at warblers. It takes too long to set up and the constantly moving birds are too hard to find with it.

What to Look For

When you first see a warbler, watch it as long as you can. It will probably be flitting in and out of cover, giving you intermittent glimpses. Each time it appears, gather as many clues as you can.

Look for Color and Patterns

It is fine to tell someone where to look on a warbler, but most of the time there is little choice. You will see what the warbler shows you and for less time than you would probably like. But if you do get a choice, here are a few priorities.

First look for any yellow, orange, or red on the bird. Many of our warblers have at least some yellow plumage, and the location and extent of the yellow can be a good clue to identification — see the Color Tab Index on the front page of the book. The absence of yellow is also a good clue.

After that, try to get a good look at the head. Many warblers have distinctive facial patterns that will help you identify them. Does the bird have an eyeline or eyebrow? Does the cheek have a distinctive pattern? Is there an eye-ring or eye crescent? Does the bird have a different-color crown?

Next look at the underparts from chin to tail. What colors are there? Is there streaking on the throat, belly, or flanks? What color is the undertail? The underparts are often what you are seeing most of, since warblers are usually high in the trees.

Then look at the wings and back. Is the back streaked or plain? What color is it? Is there a different-color rump, such as yellow? Are there wingbars, and if so, how bold are they?

Look at Behavior

There are several behaviors of warblers that can aid in identification. In no case are the behaviors definitive, but they can certainly narrow down your choices as you watch a bird. These include body movements, foraging style, and foraging height.

Body movements — There are several types of body movements that a few warbler species tend to do. Many involve the tail. Some species typically fan their tails, often highlighting patterns of white

Some Field Marks and Which Warblers Have Them

Bold Eye-ring

Canada Warbler
Chestnut-sided Warbler (fall)
Colima Warbler
Connecticut Warbler
Magnolia Warbler (fall)
Nashville Warbler
Ovenbird
Virginia's Warbler

Eyebrow

Black-and-white Warbler
Blackburnian Warbler
Black-throated Blue Warbler (female)
Black-throated Gray Warbler
Black-throated Green Warbler
Cape May Warbler
Cerulean Warbler
Golden-cheeked Warbler
Golden-winged Warbler
Grace's Warbler
Kentucky Warbler
Louisiana Waterthrush
Magnolia Warbler (spring)
Northern Waterthrush
Orange-crowned Warbler
Palm Warbler
Prairie Warbler
Tennessee Warbler
Townsend's Warbler
Worm-eating Warbler
Yellow-rumped "Myrtle" Warbler
Yellow-throated Warbler

Plain Yellow Face

Hermit Warbler
Hooded Warbler
Prothonotary Warbler
Wilson's Warbler
Yellow Warbler

Wingbar(s)

Bay-breasted Warbler
Black-and-white Warbler
Blackburnian Warbler
Blackpoll Warbler
Black-throated Gray Warbler
Black-throated Green Warbler
Blue-winged Warbler
Cape May Warbler
Cerulean Warbler
Chestnut-sided Warbler
Golden-cheeked Warbler
Golden-winged Warbler
Grace's Warbler
Hermit Warbler
Kirtland's Warbler
Magnolia Warbler
Northern Parula
Olive Warbler
Painted Redstart
Pine Warbler
Prairie Warbler
Townsend's Warbler
Tropical Parula
Yellow-rumped Warbler
Yellow-throated Warbler

Yellow Rump

Cape May Warbler
Magnolia Warbler
Palm Warbler
Virginia's Warbler
Yellow-rumped Warbler

Behaviors Typical of Certain Warbler Species

Bobs Tail

Bay-breasted Warbler
Blackpoll Warbler
Connecticut Warbler
Kirtland's Warbler
Louisiana Waterthrush
Lucy's Warbler
Nashville Warbler (mostly in West,
    some in East)

Northern Waterthrush
Palm Warbler
Pine Warbler
Prairie Warbler
Virginia's Warbler
Yellow Warbler

Waves Tail

Canada Warbler
Common Yellowthroat
Kentucky Warbler

MacGillivray's Warbler
Red-faced Warbler
Wilson's Warbler

Spreads Tail

American Redstart
Hooded Warbler

Magnolia Warbler
Painted Redstart

Walks Rather Than Hops When on Ground

Connecticut Warbler
Louisiana Waterthrush
Northern Waterthrush

Ovenbird
Swainson's Warbler

Forages on Tree Trunks

Black-and-white Warbler
Orange-crowned Warbler
Pine Warbler

Prothonotary Warbler
Yellow-throated Warbler

Flycatches

Many species of warblers flycatch (that is, fly out to catch insects in the air), but these species tend to do it the most.

American Redstart
Black-throated Blue Warbler
Black-throated Green Warbler
Canada Warbler
Hermit Warbler
Hooded Warbler

Painted Redstart
Prairie Warbler
Red-faced Warbler
Wilson's Warbler
Yellow-rumped Warbler

on their tail feathers. This behavior is especially evident in Magnolia and Hooded Warblers and in American and Painted Redstarts.

Tail bobbing is also characteristic of several species. These include Lucy's, Blackpoll, Nashville (mostly in the West, some in the East),

Palm, Prairie, and Virginia's Warblers and the two waterthrushes.

Some other warblers are tail twitchers. This means that they tend to wave their tail around or move it side to side, not just up and down like the bobbers.

A few species that feed on the ground walk rather than hop as they move. This can be a good clue to their identity. The few that walk include Connecticut and Swainson's Warblers, Ovenbird, and the two waterthrushes. Other ground-loving species usually hop.

Foraging style — Most warblers glean insects off the flowers and leaves of trees. They move about quickly as they search and rapidly inspect every surface. A few species also add flycatching to their feeding repertoire. This means that they make a short flight out to catch an airborne insect, catch it with their beak, and then return to a perch. American Redstarts and Yellow-rumped Warblers are particularly known for this.

A few warblers spend a lot of time moving about tree trunks and larger branches looking for insects in bark crevices. Some of these have slightly longer bills, enabling them to reach deeper into crevices. These include the Black-and-white Warbler particularly, which feeds this way almost exclusively (much like a nuthatch). Others that use this behavior occasionally are Orange-crowned, Prothonotary, Yellow-throated, and Pine Warblers.

Foraging height — Many warblers typically specialize in looking for food at certain heights. Some specialists are mostly on the ground, such as Ovenbird and waterthrushes. Others, like Common Yellowthroats, are usually at about 3–8 feet off the ground (about eye height for us), and still others may prefer to feed at the very top of trees, like Black-burnian, Black-throated Green, and Cape May warblers. Some warblers, like the Yellow-rumped, may feed at any height. The foraging heights of warblers are more defined on their breeding territories. During migration, they often have to take what they can get and are forced to feed in a wider variety of heights and habitats.

Learn Some Songs and Calls

Male warblers sing in spring and early summer. Some of their songs are very distinctive, easy to learn, and will alert you to a species' presence. In many other species, songs can vary tremendously. These variations sometimes start to sound much like the variations of other species, making them very difficult to tell apart.

The calls of warblers can be useful for the discerning ear. Remember that each species of warbler has several different calls in its vocal repertoire. Some are used in flight, some during feeding, others around the nest. It is not as simple as one call per warbler.

If you add all of these ways of looking at warblers to your identification skills, you will not only find it more fun to watch warblers but also easier to identify them.

Where Warblers Nest

This is an approximation of where each species tends to nest. For every species there will be quite a bit of variation.

On Ground

Black-and-white Warbler
Blue-winged Warbler
Canada Warbler
Colima Warbler
Connecticut Warbler
Golden-winged Warbler
Kentucky Warbler
Kirtland's Warbler
Louisiana Waterthrush
Mourning Warbler
Nashville Warbler

Northern Waterthrush
Tennessee Warbler
Orange-crowned Warbler
Ovenbird
Painted Redstart
Palm Warbler
Red-faced Warbler
Virginia's Warbler
Wilson's Warbler
Worm-eating Warbler

In Shrubs

Black-throated Blue Warbler
Chestnut-sided Warbler
Common Yellowthroat
Hooded Warbler
MacGillivray's Warbler

Prairie Warbler
Swainson's Warbler
Yellow-breasted Chat
Yellow Warbler

In Tree Cavity

Lucy's Warbler

Prothonotary Warbler
(also nest boxes)

In Tree, Less Than 10 Feet Up

Blackpoll Warbler

Magnolia Warbler

In Tree, 10–20 Feet Up

American Redstart
Bay-breasted Warbler
Golden-cheeked Warbler

Northern Parula
Tropical Parula
Yellow-rumped Warbler

In Tree, 20 or More Feet Up

Blackburnian Warbler
Black-throated Gray Warbler
Black-throated Green Warbler
Cape May Warbler
Cerulean Warbler
Grace's Warbler

Hermit Warbler
Olive Warbler
Pine Warbler
Townsend's Warbler
Yellow-throated Warbler

When and Where to Look for Warblers

Spring and Fall Migration

The best time to see warblers is during spring and fall migrations, and many birdwatchers look forward to these times with much anticipation. Spring warbler migration occurs mostly in April and May; fall migration can be seen from August through November. To be sure you will not miss the warblers, thumb through the guide and look at the spring and fall migration maps. They will show you the dates when each species starts its main movement through your area. Once you have a sense of this, plan to start going out looking for warblers about a

---

Spring Migration Timing in the East

Dates refer to when migrating birds first start to appear in the southern United States.

Early (Begins Before 4/1)

Black-and-white Warbler
Black-throated Green Warbler
Louisiana Waterthrush
Northern Parula
Orange-crowned Warbler
Palm Warbler
Pine Warbler
Prothonotary Warbler
Worm-eating Warbler
Yellow-rumped Warbler
Yellow-throated Warbler

Middle (Begins Between 4/1 and 4/20)

American Redstart
Blackburnian Warbler
Black-throated Blue Warbler
Blue-winged Warbler
Cape May Warbler
Cerulean Warbler
Chestnut-sided Warbler
Common Yellowthroat
Golden-winged Warbler
Hooded Warbler
Kentucky Warbler
Magnolia Warbler
Nashville Warbler
Northern Waterthrush
Ovenbird
Prairie Warbler
Swainson's Warbler
Tennessee Warbler
Wilson's Warbler
Yellow-breasted Chat
Yellow Warbler

Late (Begins After 4/20)

Bay-breasted Warbler
Blackpoll Warbler
Canada Warbler
Connecticut Warbler
Mourning Warbler

Fall Migration Timing in the East

Dates refer to when the first birds start to migrate south.

Early (Begins Before 8/1)

Cerulean Warbler	Prairie Warbler
Hooded Warbler	Worm-eating Warbler
Louisiana Waterthrush	Yellow Warbler

Middle (Begins Between 8/1 and 8/20)

American Redstart	Mourning Warbler
Black-and-white Warbler	Northern Parula
Blackburnian Warbler	Northern Waterthrush
Blackpoll Warbler	Prothonotary Warbler
Black-throated Green Warbler	Swainson's Warbler
Blue-winged Warbler	Tennessee Warbler
Canada Warbler	Wilson's Warbler
Kentucky Warbler	Yellow-breasted Chat
Magnolia Warbler	Yellow-throated Warbler

Late (Begins After 8/20)

Bay-breasted Warbler	Nashville Warbler
Black-throated Blue Warbler	Orange-crowned Warbler
Cape May Warbler	Ovenbird
Chestnut-sided Warbler	Palm Warbler
Common Yellowthroat	Pine Warbler
Connecticut Warbler	Yellow-rumped Warbler
Golden-winged Warbler	

week ahead of this time. In spring, the majority of warblers can go through some areas in 2–3 weeks. In fall, this movement occurs over several months and you have more leeway and time.

Most warblers migrate on clear nights when they have mild tail-winds. The next morning, after migrating all night, warblers are usually hungry and a little tired. They spend that morning feeding and sometimes continuing to gradually move in their migratory direction. On nights when they start out under favorable conditions and then the wind changes direction or they run into fog or storms, they are forced to drop down wherever they are. Sometimes this results in a great number of warblers all in the same area. This is called fallout, and although it is not particularly good for the birds, it is good for warbler-watching. These are the times you will see your greatest number of species and birds.

During migration, go out to look for warblers anytime from first light to about 9–10 A.M. This

Spring Migration Timing in the West

Dates refer to when migrating birds first start to appear in the southern United States.

Early (Begins Before 4/1)

Golden-cheeked Warbler	Painted Redstart
Lucy's Warbler	Tropical Parula
Olive Warbler	Wilson's Warbler
Orange-crowned Warbler	

Middle to Late (Begins Between 4/1 and 4/20)

American Redstart	Nashville Warbler
Black-throated Gray Warbler	Red-faced Warbler
Colima Warbler	Townsend's Warbler
Common Yellowthroat	Virginia's Warbler
Grace's Warbler	Yellow-breasted Chat
Hermit Warbler	Yellow Warbler
MacGillivray's Warbler	Yellow-rumped Warbler

Fall Migration Timing in the West

Dates refer to when the first birds start to migrate south.

Early (Begins Before 8/1)

Colima Warbler	Lucy's Warbler
Golden-cheeked Warbler	Yellow Warbler
Hermit Warbler	

Middle (Begins Between 8/1 and 8/20)

American Redstart	Red-faced Warbler
Black-throated Gray Warbler	Townsend's Warbler
Common Yellowthroat	Tropical Parula
Grace's Warbler	Virginia's Warbler
Nashville Warbler	Wilson's Warbler
Orange-crowned Warbler	Yellow-breasted Chat

Late (Begins After 8/20)

MacGillivray's Warbler	Palm Warbler
Olive Warbler	Yellow-rumped Warbler
Painted Redstart	

Migration Routes of Warblers

Some warblers may be included in more than one category.

Trans-Gulf

Trans-Gulf migrants fly across the Gulf of Mexico between the Yucatán Peninsula and the Gulf Coast from Texas to Florida.

American Redstart
Bay-breasted Warbler
Black-and-white Warbler
Blackburnian Warbler
Blackpoll Warbler
Black-throated Green Warbler
Blue-winged Warbler
Cerulean Warbler
Chestnut-sided Warbler
Common Yellowthroat
Golden-winged Warbler
Hooded Warbler
Kentucky Warbler
Louisiana Waterthrush

Magnolia Warbler
Northern Parula
Northern Waterthrush
Orange-crowned Warbler
Ovenbird
Prothonotary Warbler
Swainson's Warbler
Tennessee Warbler
Worm-eating Warbler
Yellow-breasted Chat
Yellow Warbler
Yellow-rumped Warbler
Yellow-throated Warbler

Circum-Gulf

Circum-Gulf migrants do not fly across the Gulf of Mexico but stick to the land, usually migrating along portions of the Gulf Coast from western Mexico to Florida.

Black-and-white Warbler
Black-throated Green Warbler
Canada Warbler
Common Yellowthroat
Mourning Warbler
Nashville Warbler
Northern Waterthrush
Orange-crowned Warbler

Ovenbird
Pine Warbler
Wilson's Warbler
Yellow-breasted Chat
Yellow Warbler
Yellow-rumped Warbler
Yellow-throated Warbler

is often when they are most active, refueling after their nightly journey. You can find birds anywhere, from center cities to the country. Any geographic or vegetative feature that forms an edge, barrier, corridor, or isolated favorable habitat is a place where warblers can be found. These include city parks, arboretums, cemeteries, coastal islands, north-south rivers, lake edges, field edges, and road edges. Be sure not to forget your own backyard. There are always a

Southeast U.S. via Florida

These migrants fly between the West Indies or northeastern South America and Florida and then into the southeastern states.

American Redstart
Black-and-white Warbler
Blackpoll Warbler
Black-throated Blue Warbler
Black-throated Green Warbler
Cape May Warbler
Common Yellowthroat
Connecticut Warbler
Kirtland's Warbler (rare)
Louisiana Waterthrush
Northern Parula

Northern Waterthrush
Orange-crowned Warbler
Ovenbird
Palm Warbler
Pine Warbler
Prairie Warbler
Swainson's Warbler
Worm-eating Warbler
Yellow-rumped Warbler
Yellow-throated Warbler

Through the West

Warblers breeding in the West often migrate north closer to the coast and migrate south farther inland, along the larger mountain ranges.

Black-throated Gray Warbler
Common Yellowthroat
Grace's Warbler
Hermit Warbler
MacGillivray's Warbler
Nashville Warbler
Orange-crowned Warbler

Townsend's Warbler
Virginia's Warbler
Wilson's Warbler
Yellow-breasted Chat
Yellow Warbler
Yellow-rumped Warbler

Along U.S.-Mexico Border Only

These are generally short-distance migrants that move between northern Mexico and southern portions of Arizona, New Mexico, and Texas.

Colima Warbler
Golden-cheeked Warbler
Lucy's Warbler
Olive Warbler

Painted Redstart
Red-faced Warbler
Tropical Parula

few warblers nearly everywhere. You never know how good your own backyard is until you take time each day during migration to look for warblers there.

Outside the migration periods you can also find warblers on their breeding and wintering grounds. The two most widespread breeding warblers are the Common Yellow-throat and the Yellow Warbler. These can be seen over most of North America in summer. Other warblers are more limited in their breeding range and you have to look through the range maps to get an idea of which ones will be breeding in your area.

The majority of warbler species leave Canada and the United States in winter, but a few regularly overwinter. These include the Pine, Palm, Yellow-rumped, and Orange-crowned Warblers and the Common Yellowthroat. These can be found in southern states and up along the East Coast.

Warbler Hotspots

It is often the case that local birders will know where to go to see warblers during migration. This is information and experience that has been passed down for decades. By contacting your local nature center or birding club, you should be able to get information on where and exactly when to look for warblers. Then it is up to the weather conditions and the birds to deliver. Sometimes these locations are so good for warblers that people travel to them from all over the country just to see warblers during migration. Some of these hotspots are:

Point Pelee National Park, Ontario — On the northern shore of Lake Erie (36 species of warblers observed annually).
Point Pelee National Park
407 Robson Street, R.R. #1
Leamington, Ontario
Canada N8H 3V4
Phone: 519-322-2365
Park info: 519-322-2371

Fax: 519-322-1277
On the Web: www.pelee.com

Mount Auburn Cemetery, Cambridge, Massachusetts
Friends of Mount Auburn
580 Mount Auburn Street
Cambridge, MA 02138
Phone: 617-547-7105
The Brookline Bird Club has field trips daily between mid-April and late May. For info, go to the BBC Web site, http://www.massbird.org/BBC/

Cape May, New Jersey
Contact: Cape May Bird Observatory
P.O. Box 3
Cape May Point, NJ 08212
Phone: 609-884-2736
Fax: 609-884-6052
On the Web: http://www.njaudubon.org

Crane Creek State Park, Ohio — On the southern shore of Lake Erie. Contact Crane Creek State Park by phone at 419-898-2495, or contact the Erie County Visitor Bureau at 800-255-3743.

High Island, Texas — A coastal Texas town that has two sanctuaries managed by the Houston Audubon Society. To contact the society:
Phone: 713-932-1639
Fax: 713-461-2911
E-mail: houstonaudubon@houston.rr.com
On the Web: http://www.houstonaudubon.org

Directions and maps to High Island are at http://www.houstonaudubon.org/highisland.html. See the paragraph entitled "Visiting the High Island Sanctuaries." Of the two sanctuaries, the better one for migrating warblers is Boy Scout Woods, along 5th Street; the other is Smith Oaks, at the end of Winnie Street.

Dauphin Island, Alabama — The 164-acre Dauphin Island Audubon Bird Sanctuary is at the eastern end of Dauphin Island, along the Gulf Coast of Alabama. Dauphin Island Park and Beach Board
109 Bienville Boulevard
Dauphin Island, AL 36528
Phone: 251-861-3607
Dauphin Island info on the Web:
http://www.gulfinfo.com/ditown

Dry Tortugas, Florida — Of these seven coral islands west of Key West, Fort Jefferson on Garden Key is the best place for warblers. Access is by boat or seaplane. For information on commercial tour operators:
National Park Service
Everglades National Park
40001 SR-9336
Homestead, FL 33034
Phone: 305-242-7700

Central Park, New York City
Central Park Conservancy
14 East 60th Street
New York, NY 10022
Phone: 212-310-6600
E-mail: contact@centralparknyc.org
On the Web: http://www.centralparknyc.org

Molts and Plumages of Warblers

Molts

When birds lose old feathers and grow new ones in their place, this is called molting. The simplest overview of molting in warblers is this: Each year in late summer, adults have a complete molt of all their feathers, resulting in the plumage we see during fall migration and winter, commonly called the fall plumage; and each year in late winter, they have a partial molt, not involving their major wing and tail feathers, resulting in the plumage we see in spring migration and summer breeding, usually called the spring plumage. This partial molt in late winter varies in extent, from just the head and throat feathers in some species to all of the body feathers in others.

In the first year of a warbler's life, the first late summer molt is different. At this time, the immature birds do not have a complete molt as the adults do, but keep their major wing and tail feathers until their second summer. In their second fall, as adults, they undergo a complete molt.

How Plumages Vary in Warblers

Warblers may look different depending on their age, sex, and whether it is spring or fall. In general, adult males have the brightest plumages, adult females are often slightly paler, and immature birds (in their first fall through the next summer) are even paler. The immature females are the palest of all.

The box on the facing page lists warbler species according to the number of adult plumages they show each year.

One plumage — More than half our warbler species have only one adult plumage. These birds look pretty much the same all year. If there are differences in appearance between the sexes or seasonally, they are minor. This is important to remember and greatly simplifies warbler identification.

Two plumages — For a few other species, there are significant differences in appearance between the adult male and female, but no seasonal change. The ones with the most obvious differences include the American Redstart, Common Yellowthroat, and Black-throated Blue and Cerulean Warblers.

For one species, there is a difference between adult spring and fall plumages but the sexes look alike. This is the Palm Warbler.

Four plumages — For six species, there is a difference in the sexes and a difference in spring and fall plumage for adults. These are the ones for which you have to remember the greatest number of plumages.

Number of Adult Plumages

Here is a list of the warblers arranged by the number of significantly different plumages they have.

One Adult Plumage

Warblers with roughly one plumage for both sexes all year.

Black-throated Gray Warbler	Ovenbird
Black-throated Green Warbler	Painted Redstart
Blue-winged Warbler	Pine Warbler
Colima Warbler	Prairie Warbler
Connecticut Warbler	Prothonotary Warbler
Golden-cheeked Warbler	Red-faced Warbler
Grace's Warbler	Swainson's Warbler
Hermit Warbler	Tennessee Warbler
Kentucky Warbler	Townsend's Warbler
Kirtland's Warbler	Tropical Parula
Louisiana Waterthrush	Virginia's Warbler
Lucy's Warbler	Wilson's Warbler
Nashville Warbler	Worm-eating Warbler
Northern Waterthrush	Yellow-breasted Chat
Orange-crowned Warbler	Yellow-throated Warbler

Two Adult Plumages

The male and female look substantially different from each other, but neither of them changes much over the course of the year.

American Redstart	Golden-winged Warbler
Black-and-white Warbler	Hooded Warbler
Blackburnian Warbler	MacGillivray's Warbler
Black-throated Blue Warbler	Mourning Warbler
Canada Warbler	Northern Parula
Cerulean Warbler	Olive Warbler
Common Yellowthroat	Yellow Warbler

Two Adult Plumages

Male and female look alike, but their spring and fall plumage are different.

Palm Warbler

Four Adult Plumages

These warblers have the greatest number of plumages. Males and females look different from each other, and both change plumage in spring and fall.

Bay-breasted Warbler	Chestnut-sided Warbler
Blackpoll Warbler	Magnolia Warbler
Cape May Warbler	Yellow-rumped Warbler

Acknowledgments

We would like to thank all of the photographers who participated in this book for the use of their beautiful slides. We also would like to thank Kevin Karlson and Michael O'Brien for reading over the manuscript and making many helpful suggestions and corrections. Any errors that may inadvertently be in this book are solely the responsibility of the authors.

Photo Credits

Photographs are listed by page number and then page position, with A being at the top and going downward with B, C, and D as needed.

Ron Austing: 36A, 37A, 97A, 97C, 121A, 131A.

Rick and Nora Bowers: 75C, 75D, 123A, 127A.

Herbert Clarke: 59C, 83D, 87B, 105A, 107B, 135B, 139C, 163A.

Rob Curtis: 73C.

Mike Danzenbaker: 115D, 155A, 155B, 161A.

Roger Eriksson: 49D, 55D, 79B, 79C, 80B, 81A, 81B, 111A, 113C, 113D, 119C, 133D, 147C, 147D, 149A, 161B.

Jim Flynn: 51D, 139D, 160.

Kevin Karlson: 13, 14A, 14B, 47B, 51C, 53C, 55B, 57C, 63C, 67B, 69C, 69D, 71B, 71D, 83B, 89A, 91C, 115A, 115C, 128A, 131C, 131D, 133A, 133B, 137A, 141A, 145B, 149B, 151A, 153A, 162.

Maslowski Photo: 107A, 121B.

Anthony Mercieca: 49B, 49C, 51B, 57B, 61C, 109A, 115B, 125A, 125B, 149C.

Photo Researchers, Inc. — Adam Jones: 69B; Thomas W. Martin: 69A, 128B.

Clair Postmus: 36B, 37C, 43C, 53A, 61A, 89B, 97B, 117D.

Robert Royse: 43A, 47A, 49A, 51A, 55A, 57A, 61B, 63B, 63D, 73A, 73B, 75A, 75B, 79A, 83A, 85A, 91A, 91B, 101B, 101D, 103A, 103B, 111B, 117A, 119D, 131B, 139A, 143A, 143B, 151C.

Larry Sansone: 39A, 43D, 47C, 73D, 105B, 117C, 151B, 153B.

Brian Small: 37D, 38A, 38B, 38C, 39B, 39C, 43B, 45A, 45B, 47D, 53B, 53D, 55C, 59A, 59B, 59D, 63A, 65A, 65B, 71A, 71C, 77A, 77B, 83C, 85B, 87A, 93, 95, 99A, 99B, 99C, 99D, 101A, 101C, 103C, 103D, 105C, 109B, 110, 113A, 113B, 117B, 119A, 119B, 123B, 127B, 129, 135A, 135C, 137B, 137C, 139B, 141B, 145A, 147A, 147B, 156, 158, 159A, 163B.

Tom Vezo: 36C, 37B, 67A, 80A, 89C, 91D, 97D, 133C, 159B, 161C.

Start Here by Learning Yellow-rumped Warblers

Yellow-rumped Warblers are the most abundant warbler during fall migration, winter, and spring migration. In fall and winter, as many as 80–90 percent of the warblers seen can be Yellow-rumps. So if you learn to identify Yellow-rumps really well, it will help you pick out a warbler that is different. In fact, when you see a warbler in fall, winter, or spring, your first question should be: "Why is this not a Yellow-rumped Warbler?"

Year-round Identification Clues

There are several good clues to Yellow-rumps throughout the year. Here are the best ones.

- **Bright yellow rump:** This is best seen when the bird faces away, droops its wings, or flies. It can be hidden by the wings at other times.

- **Yellow patches on either side of breast, just before wing:** These are seen on all Yellow-rumps in spring and summer and on 90–95 percent of the birds in fall and winter. The other 5–10 percent in fall and winter are immature females with little or no yellow on the sides.

- **Split eye-ring and dark face:** All plumages of Yellow-rumps show a split white eye-ring. This looks like thin white arcs above and below the eyes. The face and cheeks are either dark brown, gray, or black, but always dark.

- **Streaked back and flanks:** The back is always dark (either brown or gray) and streaked. And the flanks are always streaked with black or brown over a whitish background.

- **White undertail coverts:** The feathers that cover the base of the tail are always white.

Additional Fall and Winter Clues

In fall and winter, Yellow-rumps are pretty dull birds — mostly brown above and streaked brown below. The throat is either dull white or yellow.

There is a great deal of individual variation in fall Yellow-rumps, making it hard to confidently tell the age or sex of a bird. In general, adult males will have the most contrast in their plumage (darker areas being more gray-brown) and immature females will be the dullest (dark areas all pale brown). The rest (adult females and immature males) are in between.

Additional Spring Clues

All Yellow-rumps are more colorful in spring.

Males change the most and become quite colorful. They have a gray head and back, a yellow crown patch, brighter yellow patches on the sides of their breast, a black mask, and variable black patches or black streaking on breast and flanks.

The females are similar to males, but their back and head are more brownish, the mask on their face is grayish, and the black on their breast and flanks is less extensive.

Don't Forget Behavior

Behavior is a wonderful aid and added confirmation to identification. Although any one behavior is rarely a clincher, behaviors in the aggregate can strongly suggest an identification. Here are some behaviors of Yellow-rumped Warblers that can help you out.

Often in Flocks

This is one of our few warbler species that actually makes a habit of migrating and wintering in flocks. The flocks can range from a few birds to hundreds. Often, other warbler species are mixed in with these flocks, so scan through the flocks looking for the few that are different.

Winter Warbler

Because it has a wide variety of feeding methods and because it eats berries, the Yellow-rump can survive through winter in many of the Lower 48 states. Its main food at this time is berries — bayberry, wax myrtle, poison ivy, et cetera. This helps make it the most common and widespread winter warbler.

Varied Feeding Behavior

The Yellow-rump is a real general-ist among the warblers. It feeds from high in the treetops as well as on the ground. It can sally out to catch insects like a flycatcher and it can creep around tree trunks in search of insects. It also gleans in-sects off leaves like many other warblers. It is one of the few war-blers to eat fruit and thus can be seen near sources of berries. When feeding it is usually very active and often twitches its tail.

Aggressive Behavior

Yellow-rumps tend to engage in chases of their own species, espe-cially during migration.

"Myrtle" versus "Audubon's" Warblers

There are two subspecies of Yellow-rumped Warblers that used to be considered different species. They are designated the "Myrtle" and "Audubon's" Yellow-rumps. There is no need for the average birder to use these names, for it is assumed that if you say "Yellow-rumped Warbler" and you are in the East, you mean "Myrtle," and if you are in the West, you mean "Audubon's," since this is gener-ally how these subspecies are dis-tributed.

The easiest way to tell them apart is to look at the head. "Myr-tles" have a pale to white eyebrow, giving their face more pattern; "Audubon's" have no eyebrow, and so their face looks very uni-form and plain. Also, "Myrtles" al-ways have a whitish throat; "Audubon's" usually have a pale to dark yellow throat (except for some fall immature females, which can have no yellow on the throat).

The following pages highlight the identifying features of these two subspecies.

"Myrtle" adult male, spring:
Look for distinctive yellow patches on sides of breast. Yellow rump and crown also visible on this bird. The black mask and white throat make this a spring adult male "Myrtle."

"Myrtle" adult female, spring:
Look for distinctive yellow patches on sides of breast. The charcoal to brownish mask and white throat make this a spring adult female "Myrtle."

"Myrtle," fall: Look for distinctive yellow patches on sides of breast — they are always present in adults, although sometimes reduced in fall. Note whitish eyebrow and brownish overall appearance.

"Myrtle," fall: The distinctive yellow patches can be quite reduced in fall adult females. Note the eyebrow, split eye-ring, and brownish breast streaking seen in all fall "Myrtles."

"Myrtle," fall: The yellow rump, overall brownish appearance, whitish eyebrow, and split eye-ring still identify this as a Yellow-rump. A hint of yellow patch barely shows on side of breast.

"Myrtle," fall: Even at this angle the yellow rump, streaked back, and facial pattern identify this as a Yellow-rump.

"Myrtle," fall: The dullest of all plumages, with no yellow patches showing on breast. Still, the whitish eyebrow, split eye-ring, and brown streaking on breast and flanks help identify the bird as a "Myrtle." Yellow rump is there but hidden. This is probably an immature female.

"Audubon's" adult male, spring: The distinctive yellow throat and yellow patches on the side of the breast are clear on this spring adult male. Note that the face is plainer than that of a "Myrtle," having no eyebrow and no dark mask.

"Audubon's" adult female, spring: The distinctive yellow throat and yellow patches on the sides of the breast are clear but smaller on this spring adult female. Note that the face is plainer than that of a "Myrtle," having no eyebrow and no dark mask.

"Audubon's," fall: The distinctive yellow throat and yellow patches on the sides of the breast are still clear. Note that the breast is now streaked gray and not black as in spring.

"Audubon's," fall: The yellow rump is just visible, as are the yellow on the throat and side of the breast. Note the ever-present split eye-ring and streaking on the back.

"Audubon's," fall: All the distinctive yellow markings on this bird are paler and reduced.

"Audubon's," fall: This is the plainest of all the plumages. There is the slightest glimpse of the yellow rump, but the yellow on the throat and sides of the breast is barely visible or lacking. This is probably an immature female.

Identification
Pages

Yellow Warbler

Dendroica petechia   4.75"

Main Year-round Clues

- All-yellow warbler.
- Only warbler with mostly yellow underside of tail.
- Yellow edges to all wing feathers.
- See also Behavior.

Additional Clues

MALE: Reddish streaks on breast.
FEMALE: Duller yellow, with breast streaking faint or absent.
IMMATURES IN FALL: Duskier plumage; can be all pale olive. Still has distinctive yellowish undertail.

Voice

Song sounds like "sweet sweet sweet sweeter than sweet" or "sweet sweet sweet sweet." *East: Disk 3, track 11.*

Undertail Pattern

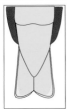

Undertail coverts yellow; tail mostly yellow on underside.

Behavior and Habitat

Often bobs tail. Can be found in yards and gardens. Common all across N. America. Breeds in shrubby areas, especially near water and with alders and/or willows.

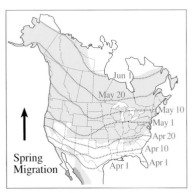

Migration in the East is across or around the Gulf of Mexico. Migration period is prolonged.

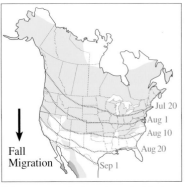

Migratory population winters in Mexico to Cent. and S. America. Western birds generally migrate later than eastern birds.

Male

Female

Female

Fall immature

Orange-crowned Warbler, Western

Vermivora celata 5"

Western Subspecies (Eastern Subspecies on p. 148)

Main Year-round Clues

Undertail Pattern

- Lack of distinctive field marks.
- Dull yellow to olive underparts; dull olive upperparts.
- Yellow undertail coverts always the brightest part of the bird.
- Indistinct streaking on breast.
- Split eye-ring.
- Faint dark eyeline.
- Orange crown usually concealed.

Undertail coverts yellow; no spots on grayish tail.

Additional Clues

IMMATURES: Imm. females are mostly dull yellow on breast and belly; yellow undertail coverts.

Voice

Song is a high-pitched trill that trails off at the end. *East: Disk 3, track 8.*

Behavior and Habitat

When foraging, moves more slowly than most warblers. Feeds mostly low in underbrush and understory. May come to suet, seed, or hummingbird feeders in winter. Breeds in dense thickets, forest edges, brushy fields.

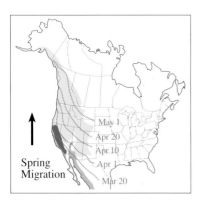

Western birds migrate much earlier than eastern birds.

One subspecies breeds only on Channel Islands of Calif., winters in coastal Calif.

Adult

Immature

Prothonotary Warbler

Protonotaria citrea   5.5"

Main Year-round Clues

- Golden yellow face and underparts.
- Unmarked blue-gray wings.
- Blue-gray tail with white tail spots at base.
- Green back.
- Relatively long bill and short tail.

Additional Clues

MALE: Bright golden head.
FEMALE AND IMMATURES: Variable olive tinge on crown and face; yellow duller.

Voice

Song a long series of loud notes on one pitch: "sweet sweet sweet sweet sweet."
East: Disk 3, track 30.

Undertail Pattern

Undertail coverts white; tail relatively short and mostly white but dark at tip.

Behavior and Habitat

Moves leisurely when feeding. Breeds in swampy woods. Nests in tree holes.

Migration is across Gulf of Mexico. Single males often appear in spring north of the breeding range. Found in wooded areas in or next to water.

Winters in Cent. and S. America, where it is typically found in mangrove swamps.

Male

Male

Female

First-spring
female

Blue-winged Warbler

Vermivora pinus 4.75"

Main Year-round Clues

- Bright yellow underparts with white undertail coverts.
- Black line from eye to bill.
- Two whitish wingbars on blue-gray wings.

Additional Clues

ADULT MALE: Yellow crown. Brighter underparts, darker eyeline, and bolder white wingbars than females and imm.
ADULT FEMALE AND IMMATURES: Variable olive tinge on crown. Wingbars thinner, eyeline not as dark as on adult male.
HYBRIDS: Blue-winged and Golden-winged Warblers sometimes interbreed, creating hybrids that share traits of both species. These hybrids may then breed with either species. This creates a host of variations in plumage. First-generation hybrids are usually called "Brewster's" Warbler (shown at right), while second-generation hybrids (backcrosses) are sometimes called "Lawrence's" Warbler (see p. 101).

Undertail Pattern

Undertail coverts white; large white tail spots.

Voice

Song is 2 buzzy low-pitched notes, second note usually lower and rougher. Sounds like "bzay bzeee." Hybrids can sing the song of either parent or a mixture of both. *East: Disk 3, track 5.*

Behavior and Habitat

Prefers forest edges and open areas with dense undergrowth during breeding and migration. Also abandoned orchards.

Spring Migration

May 10
May 1
Apr 20
Apr 10
Apr 1

Fall Migration

Aug 10
Aug 20
Sep 1
Sep 10

Winters in Mexico and Cent. America; migration is across Gulf of Mexico. Breeding range is expanding northward.

Breeds in open shrubby or weedy areas such as power line cuts, but migrants may use woodlands and wooded edges.

Male

Female

Fall immature
female

"Brewster's"
Warbler
(hybrid)

Pine Warbler

Dendroica pinus 5.25"

Main Year-round Clues

- Yellow from throat to breast or belly.
- Large warbler, usually on pines.
- Plain unstreaked upperparts olive to brownish olive; 2 white wingbars.
- Black legs.
- Long tail with distinct notch at tip.
- See also Behavior.

Undertail coverts white; white tail spots on underside of tail.

Additional Clues

MALE: Yellow throat, breast, and belly; bright olive-green above; indistinct streaking on sides of breast.
FEMALE: Like adult male, but yellow limited to throat and upper breast; less streaking on sides of breast.
IMMATURES: Male similar to adult female; female grayish brown above; only pale yellow on breast, otherwise grayish. A few imm. females can be grayish overall.

Voice

Song is a musical trill on one pitch. *East: Disk 3, track 21.*

Behavior and Habitat

Often feeds by clinging to bark of trunks and branches. Usually feeds high in trees; may also feed on the ground in open areas, especially in winter. Comes to feeders for sunflower seed and suet in winter. Breeds in pines of all kinds.

Usually the first warbler to arrive in North. Details of migration not well known due to birds' year-round presence in much of their range.

The only warbler whose main winter range is within U.S. A few remain within summer range throughout winter, often come to feeders for suet.

Male

Female

Fall immature

Fall immature
female

Wilson's Warbler

Wilsonia pusilla   4.75"

Main Year-round Clues

- All yellow underneath; olive above.
- Small black to olive cap on crown.
- Small bird with slender tail and small bill.
- See also Behavior.

Additional Clues

MALE: Pure black cap.
FEMALE: Cap varies from a mixture of black and dark olive to all dark olive.
IMMATURES: Male like adult female. Female may have olive crown and forehead.

Voice

Song is a chattering descending trill. *East: Disk 3, track 41.*

Undertail Pattern

Yellow undertail coverts; no white tail spots on grayish tail feathers.

Behavior and Habitat

Very active; frequently twitches tail about and flicks wings. Often stays low in undergrowth. Breeds in dense shrubby areas, often near water, such as bogs or willow and alder thickets. More common in West than in East.

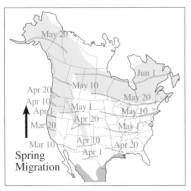

Three separate subspecies; each has its own basically distinct migration path. West Coast birds migrate earliest.

Winters in Mexico and Cent. America; some also stay in coastal Tex. and La.

Male

Male

Female

Fall immature
female

Hooded Warbler

Wilsonia citrina   5.25"

Main Year-round Clues

Undertail Pattern

Undertail coverts yellow; undertail mostly white.

- Olive above; yellow below.
- Black hood surrounds yellow face.
- Extensive white in outer tail feathers shows as bird frequently flicks open its tail.
- See also Behavior.

Additional Clues

MALE: Extensive black hood.
FEMALE: Hood varies from as extensive as male's to just an outline, with "typical" being a thin black border to yellow facial area.

Voice

Song is loud, musical, paired notes, like "ta-wee ta-wee ta-weeyo." *East: Disk 3, track 40.*

Behavior and Habitat

Flicks its tail open constantly. Feeds mostly near ground, sometimes on ground. Breeds in dense shrubbery of mature deciduous woodlands, especially near streams.

Uses traditional cross-Gulf migration path, arriving on coasts of eastern Tex. and southwestern La.

Migration path farther east than in spring, but birds still cross Gulf of Mexico. Winters in Mexico and Cent. America.

Male

Male

Female

Immature
female

Kentucky Warbler

Oporornis formosus   5.25"

Main Year-round Clues

- Bright yellow underparts.
- Bold yellow "spectacles" — a yellow line from base of bill up and around behind the eyes.
- Plain olive back and wings.
- See also Behavior.

Additional Clues

MALE: Crown and triangular mark under eye are black.
FEMALE AND IMMATURES: Black areas reduced or greenish.

Voice

Song a rolling series of 2-syllable, low-pitched notes, like "churee, churee, churee." Similar to Carolina Wren's, but not as melodic. *East: Disk 3, track 36.*

Undertail Pattern

Undertail coverts yellow and long; tail relatively short.

Behavior and Habitat

Feeds mostly on ground, where it hops or runs (does not walk). Tail often cocked, occasionally flicked. Flips fallen leaves as it looks for food. Breeds in ravines and bottomlands of moist woods.

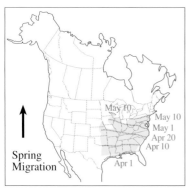

Migrates around or across Gulf and lands between E. Tex. and W. Fla. "Overshoots" occur north of breeding range each spring.

Winter range is in Mexico and Cent. America. Birds are difficult to see, foraging on or near ground in dense foliage.

Male

Male

Female

57

Nashville Warbler

Vermivora ruficapilla   4.5"

Main Year-round Clues

- Underparts all yellow except for patch of white at base of legs.
- Gray head with bold white eye-ring.
- Greenish back and wings.
- See also Behavior.

Additional Clues

MALE: Head blue-gray, underparts a rich yellow.
FEMALE: Head a muted gray, underparts a duller yellow.
IMMATURES: Whitish throat; paler yellow underparts. Belly may be white.

Voice

Song starts with a repeated phrase that is then followed by a short trill, like "see-it see-it see-it, tititititi." *East: Disk 3, track 9.*

Undertail Pattern

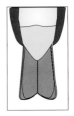

Undertail coverts yellow; no spots on tail.

Behavior and Habitat

Western subspecies typically bobs tail; eastern subspecies does so less distinctly. Breeds in open second-growth woods, thickets, woodland edges.

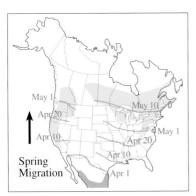

Eastern subspecies migrates around Gulf of Mexico; migrants rare in southeastern U.S. Western subspecies goes through Ariz. and Calif.

Eastern subspecies winters in E. Mexico and part of Cent. America; western subspecies winters in W. Mexico and Cent. America.

Male

Male

Female

Fall immature

Canada Warbler

Wilsonia canadensis   5.25"

Main Year-round Clues

- Yellow underparts with short streaks across breast; white undertail coverts.
- Whitish eye-ring; yellow line from bill to eye.
- Gray upperparts and no wingbars.

Additional Clues

MALE: Distinct black streaked necklace across breast. Black on crown and face.
FEMALE: Less obvious streaks across breast. No black on face or crown.
IMMATURES: Male like adult female. Female may have very little streaking on breast.

Voice

Song is a musical warbling that starts with a distinct and separate, but often quiet, "chip" note. *East: Disk 3, track 42.*

Undertail Pattern

White undertail coverts; no spots on grayish tail.

Behavior and Habitat

Tail is often cocked. Breeds in dense understory of mature deciduous and mixed woodlands, and in shrubby areas near streams and swamps.

Most migrate around western edge of Gulf of Mexico, but some fly across Gulf to easternmost Tex. and southwest La.

Migrants are usually found in dense shrubbery or brush. Rarely a vagrant. Winters in northern S. America.

Male

Male

Female

Magnolia Warbler

Dendroica magnolia   4.75″

Main Year-round Clues

♦ Bright yellow underparts with black streaking.
♦ Basal half of tail appears whitish from below; tail is often fanned, revealing white tail band.
♦ White wingbars and yellow rump.
♦ See also Behavior.

Additional Clues

SPRING MALE: Heavy black streaking on breast and belly; black face mask; white patch on wing.
SPRING FEMALE: More muted colors; less streaking beneath; 2 wingbars rather than a patch.
FALL ADULTS: Sexes similar. Head grayish with thin white eye-ring and no white eyebrow; less streaking beneath than on spring adults.
FALL IMMATURES: Similar to fall adults; less streaking beneath; no black streaking on back.

Undertail Pattern

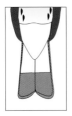

Undertail coverts white; basal half of tail whitish, other half black.

Voice

Song is a short series of musical notes, like "weety weety weety, wee." *East: Disk 3, track 13.*

Behavior and Habitat

An active feeder that often fans tail. Breeds in coniferous forests, especially thickets of spruce, hemlock, and balsam fir. Most abundant in early growth habitats.

From wintering grounds in Mexico, Cent. America, and West Indies, migrates across Gulf of Mexico.

A more eastern route than in spring; thus, birds are more common along S.E. coast of U.S. but less common on W. Gulf Coast.

Spring male

Spring male

Spring female

Fall immature

63

Townsend's Warbler

Dendroica townsendi   4.75"

Main Year-round Clues

- ◆ Yellow breast and white belly; dark streaking along flanks.
- ◆ Dark cheek patch is surrounded by yellow face.
- ◆ Two white wingbars.

Undertail Pattern

Undertail coverts white with fine black streaks; extensive white on underside of tail.

Additional Clues

MALE: Crown, throat, and ear patch black; prominent streaking on back.
FEMALE: Similar to adult male but less black on crown, back, face, and throat.
IMMATURES: Imm. male in fall and imm. female in fall and spring may have no black on throat and little or no streaking on back.

Behavior and Habitat

Feeds on insects and spiders. May come to feeders for suet, nuts, and fruit. Breeds in moist mature coniferous woods.

Voice

Song is 5–6 buzzy high-pitched "zee" notes, with 2–3 higher buzzy notes at end. *West: Disk 4, track 29a.*

Migrants found in flowering oaks and chaparral. Birds wintering in U.S. begin migrating about 2 weeks before those from farther south.

More widespread than in spring. Some winter along U.S. Pacific Coast, and some winter in Cent. America.

Male

Female

Prairie Warbler

Dendroica discolor   4.5"

Main Year-round Clues

- Yellow face and underparts; pale yellow undertail coverts. Olive above.
- Distinctive yellow crescent under eye bordered below by a darker crescent.
- Two whitish to yellow wingbars.
- Usually shows distinct streaks down sides.
- See also Behavior.

Additional Clues

MALE: Dark markings on face are black; streaking on flanks and sides of chest is bold.

FEMALE: Dark markings on face are grayish; streaking on flanks and sides of chest is thinner and reduced.

IMMATURES: Male similar to adult female. Female has pale markings on face but still shows basic pattern of adults.

Undertail Pattern

Undertail coverts pale yellow; large white tail spots.

Voice

Song is a rising series of buzzy notes. *East: Disk 3, track 23.*

Behavior and Habitat

Bobs tail a lot. Very active as it gleans insects off leaves. Breeds in brushy fields, orchards, young pine plantations, mangrove swamps.

May 10
May 1
Apr 20
Apr 10
Apr 1

Spring Migration

Migrates over Atlantic to southeastern coast of U.S., and then northwestward; few birds cross Gulf, so species is rare along Gulf Coast.

Jul 20
Aug 1
Aug 10

Fall Migration

Winters in the West Indies and Bahamas. A few are year-round residents in mangroves of coastal south Florida.

Male

Female

Palm Warbler, Eastern "Yellow Palm"

Dendroica palmarum   5"

Eastern Subspecies (Western Subspecies on p. 88)

Main Year-round Clues

- Brownish above, dark streaks over extensive yellow below.
- Bright yellow undertail coverts.
- Dark eyeline; yellow to tan eyebrow.
- Dark cheek.
- See also Behavior.

Additional Clues

SPRING: Chestnut crown. Underparts all bright yellow; strong rufous streaking on breast and flank.

FALL: Brown streaked crown. Dull yellow underparts; streaking on breast and flanks brownish and indistinct.

Voice

Song is a buzzy trill that may rise at end. *East: Disk 3, track 24.*

Undertail Pattern

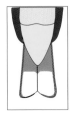

Undertail coverts bright yellow; white spots on underside of tail.

Behavior and Habitat

Constantly bobs tail as it feeds on or near the ground. Hops or runs (does not walk). Breeds in bogs near spruces. On migration and in winter, often seen feeding on the ground in grassy or weedy areas.

Two subspecies: "Yellow" breeds from central Quebec east, "Western" in rest of range. "Yellow" an earlier migrant than "Western."

Winter range is the southeast U.S. and along Gulf Coast of Tex.

Spring

Spring

Fall

Fall

Cape May Warbler

Dendroica tigrina   *4.75"*

Main Year-round Clues

- Yellow on face, breast, and rump.
- Finely streaked from breast through belly.
- Thin eyeline.
- Thin, slightly downcurved, sharply-pointed bill.
- Wing feathers have greenish edges.
- Short tail.

Additional Clues

MALE: Chestnut-orange ear patch surrounded by yellow. Black streaks on yellow underparts; white wing patch.
FEMALE: Ear patch grayish yellow, surrounded by brighter yellow. Two thin whitish wingbars; pale yellow below with faint streaking.
FALL: Adults similar to spring plumage but paler.
IMMATURES: Fall female a very pale version of adult.

Undertail Pattern

Undertail coverts tinged yellow near belly, whiter near tail. Has white tail spots. Short-tailed appearance.

Voice

Song is a very high-pitched "seet seet seet seet." *East: Disk 3, track 14.*

Behavior and Habitat

May defend sources of nectar or fruits during migration. May come to hummingbird feeders and suet in winter. Breeds in coniferous woods, spruce bogs.

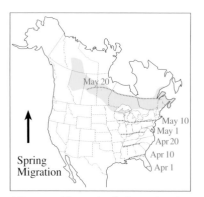

Migrates to Fla. peninsula from wintering grounds in Bahamas; sometimes found in flowering trees, eating nectar from blossoms.

Fall migration more easterly than in spring, so birds are more common along Atlantic Coast but uncommon in interior S.E.

Male

Female

Female

Fall immature
female

Connecticut Warbler

Oporornis agilis   5.5"

Main Year-round Clues

- Yellow belly and undertail coverts.
- Brown or gray hood with complete bold white eye-ring.
- Appears short-tailed because undertail coverts are long.
- Large warbler.
- See also Behavior.

Additional Clues

MALE: Gray hood.
FEMALE AND IMMATURES: Browner hood; buffy throat.

Voice

Song is halting, loud, repeated phrases, a little like "Connect-i-cut, Connect-i-cut, Connect-i-cut." *East: Disk 3, track 37.*

Undertail Pattern

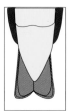

Undertail coverts yellow and long; relatively short tail.

Behavior and Habitat

Walks on ground (does not hop), bobbing head and occasionally tail. Secretive. Breeds in spruce and tamarack bogs, open poplar woods, willow scrub, and young jack pine stands.

Migration poorly known due to difficulty of finding migrants. Apparently birds cross Caribbean to Fla., then head north-westward.

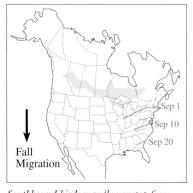

Southbound birds may fly nonstop from New England or the mid-Atlantic Coast to S. America, where they winter.

Male

Male

Male

Fall immature
female

Mourning Warbler

Oporornis philadelphia   5.25"

Main Year-round Clues

- Bright yellow belly and undertail.
- Grayish hood.
- Olive back.
- No wingbars.
- See also Behavior.

Additional Clues

MALE: Gray hood with variable black bib. No eye-ring.
FEMALE: Pale gray hood with no black on chest. Very thin eye-ring that may be broken or (rarely) complete.
IMMATURES: Yellowish throat and underparts. Broken eye-ring thicker than adult female's, but still thin.

Voice

Song is a loud series of 2-syllable phrases, with ending phrases lower-pitched. Call is a harsh "jit." *East: Disk 4, track 38.*

Undertail Pattern

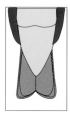

Undertail coverts yellow; no spots on short tail.

Behavior and Habitat

Hops along ground (Connecticut Warbler walks) as it looks for insects and spiders. Skulking. Breeds in dense undergrowth of second-growth habitats.

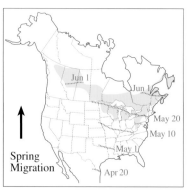

Migrates up the coast through eastern Mexico and south Tex. One of the latest warblers to arrive in spring.

Somewhat more widespread in Southeast than in spring. Winters in S. America and southern Cent. America.

Male

Male

Female

First-spring
female

MacGillivray's Warbler
Oporornis tolmiei   5.25"

Main Year-round Clues

♦ Yellow belly and undertail coverts.
♦ Gray to brownish-green hood.
♦ Olive back.
♦ Bold white crescents above and below eye.
♦ See also Behavior.

Additional Clues

MALE: Bluish-gray hood; black lores; black mottled area on chin and throat.
FEMALE: Pale gray hood with no black on throat or chest.
IMMATURES: Pale olive hood.

Voice

Song is several buzzy notes, the last ones lower-pitched. Call is a loud "tsik." *West: Disk 4, track 32b.*

Undertail Pattern

Undertail coverts short and yellow; no spots on longish tail.

Behavior and Habitat

Generally feeds in underbrush near ground; when on ground, hops (Connecticut Warbler walks) as it looks for insects and spiders. Skulking. Breeds in dense understory of mountain forests or scrubby hillsides.

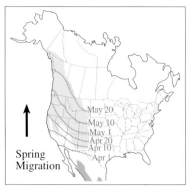

Migrants can be found in open, desert scrub habitat, although they breed in dense, shrubby areas such as old clear-cuts or burns.

Winters in Mexico and Cent. America. Migrates along Rocky Mountains; vagrants found in the East.

Male

Female

Kirtland's Warbler

Dendroica kirtlandii   5.5"

Main Year-round Clues

- Note limited range.
- Yellow from chin through belly; white undertail.
- Streaked flanks and sides of breast.
- Upperparts bluish to brownish gray with dark streaks on the back and head.
- Thin white crescents above and below eye.
- See also Behavior.

Additional Clues

MALE: Bluish-gray upperparts; black between eye and bill.
FEMALE: Brownish-gray upperparts; no black between eye and bill.
IMMATURES: Very similar to adult female; more strongly washed with brown on upperparts.

Undertail Pattern

Undertail coverts white; small white tail spots.

Voice

Song starts as a series of loud, low-pitched notes, rising in pitch and volume at the end. *East: Disk 3, track 22.*

Behavior and Habitat

A large, slow-moving warbler; often bobs tail, quickly down, then slowly up. Feeds near pines, on or near the ground. Breeds in young jack pine stands.

Spring Migration

May 10

Fall Migration

Aug 20

Probably winters only in Bahamas and migrates to coastal S.C. Birds then apparently cross N.C., Va., W.V., and Ohio on the way to Mich.

Inland migration to and from breeding grounds not well understood, as migrants are rarely seen. Fall migration apparently on same path as spring.

Male

Male

Female

Blackpoll Warbler, fall

For main species account, see p. 132.

Olive-green above, yellowish on breast and flanks. Legs yellowish, at least on back side, and soles of feet yellow. Strong eyeline. Edges of tertials are white. Undertail coverts and belly also white. Variably streaked on flanks and sides of breast. Most fall birds not reliably aged or sexed in the field.

Fall

Fall

Tennessee Warbler, fall

For main species account, see p. 146.

Pale yellow to yellow underneath except for white undertail coverts. Dark eyeline and thin pale eyebrow above. Olive-green above. May have faint thin yellow wingbars. Many fall adult females and immatures not reliably distinguished in the field.

Fall adult female or immature

Fall adult female or immature

Common Yellowthroat

Geothlypis trichas   5"

Main Year-round Clues

- Yellow throat and undertail coverts.
- Olive to olive-brown back.
- Belly yellow to whitish, varying geographically.
- See also Behavior.

Additional Clues

MALE: Black mask with a grayish band across the top. Olive crown, back, and wings.
FEMALE: No mask. Olive-brown head and upperparts.
IMMATURES: Male may have hint of black mask. Female like adult but with brownish wash to underparts.

Voice

Song is a repeated 3-part phrase, like "wichety wichety wichety." Call is a loud "tchat." *East: Disk 3, track 39.*

Undertail Pattern

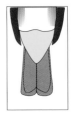

Yellow undertail coverts; no spots on dark tail.

Behavior and Habitat

Tail is usually cocked and often flicked as bird feeds on or near the ground in underbrush. Usually pops up to see what is going on, then drops into cover. Breeds in moist shrubby areas.

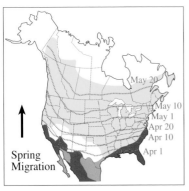

An abundant and widespread warbler; both spring and fall migration paths span the continent. Many cross the Gulf of Mexico.

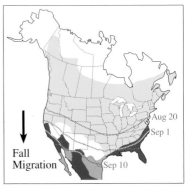

Winters in U.S., Mexico, Cent. America, and West Indies.

Male

Female

Fall immature
male

Fall immature
female

Yellow-throated Warbler

Dendroica dominica   5″

Main Year-round Clues

- Bright yellow throat and upper breast bordered by a black face and black streaking on sides.
- White eyebrow, sometimes with yellow dash near eye.
- Relatively long-billed.
- See also Behavior.

Additional Clues

ADULTS: Sexes similar. Male has more black on crown and darker streaks on flanks.

Voice

Song is a descending series of whistles that usually ends with a higher note. *East: Disk 3, track 20.*

Undertail Pattern

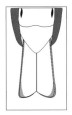

Undertail coverts white; extensive white on underside of tail.

Behavior and Habitat

Creeps leisurely along trunks and branches looking for insects to eat. Common along river floodplains; likes oak woodlands, pine forests, sycamore-cypress swamps, floodplain swamps.

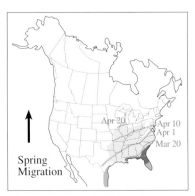

Migrates across the Gulf of Mexico and through Florida. Breeding range is expanding northward into New York and New England.

Winters in S.C., Ga., Fla., the West Indies, and Cent. America; a few also winter along mid-Atlantic Coast. Sometimes comes to bird feeders.

Male

Female

Grace's Warbler

Dendroica graciae 4.75"

Main Year-round Clues

- Bright yellow throat and upper breast.
- Broad yellow eyebrow; gray cheek.
- Black streaking on flanks.
- Gray back.

Additional Clues

ADULTS: Sexes very similar. Female may have more grayish facial markings and forehead.
IMMATURES: Like adult female but also may have buffy wash on flanks.

Voice

Song is variable whistled notes that rise in a trill at the end. *West: Disk 4, track 30.*

Undertail Pattern

Undertail coverts white; extensive white on underside of tail.

Behavior and Habitat

Does most foraging in pines. Breeds in mountain pine-oak forests.

Migrants are rarely seen; species has never been recorded east of Colo. and west Tex. Breeds in mountainous pine woods.

Winters in Cent. America, but range is uncertain because 2 subspecies are year-round residents there.

Male

Male

Palm Warbler, "Western Palm"

Dendroica palmarum   5"

Western Subspecies (Eastern Subspecies on p. 68)

Main Year-round Clues

- Brownish above, streaked below.
- Bright yellow undertail coverts.
- Dark eyeline; yellow to tan eyebrow.
- Dark cheek.
- See also Behavior.

Additional Clues

SPRING: Bright yellow chin and undertail coverts; rufous crown; variable pale yellow on belly; brown streaks on breast.
FALL: Dull brownish overall except for yellow undertail coverts and yellowish rump; less distinct streaking on breast.

Voice

Song is a buzzy trill that may rise at end. *East: Disk 3, track 24.*

Undertail Pattern

Undertail coverts bright yellow; white spots on underside of tail.

Behavior and Habitat

Constantly bobs tail as it feeds on or near the ground. Hops or runs (does not walk). Breeds in bogs near spruces. On migration and in winter, often seen feeding on the ground in grassy or weedy areas.

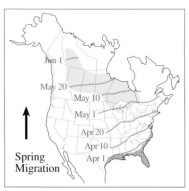

Two subspecies: "Yellow" breeds from central Quebec east, "Western" in rest of range.

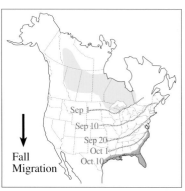

Often seen in Calif. during fall migration.

Spring

Fall

Fall

Northern Parula
Parula americana   4.25"

Main Year-round Clues

- Bright yellow throat and breast with variable darker band across the chest.
- Blue to gray above with greenish patch on upper back.
- Two bold white wingbars, and white crescents above and below the eyes.
- Very small, short-tailed warbler.

Additional Clues

MALE: Band on chest often black at upper edge and chestnut on lower edge.
FEMALE: Chestband faint.
IMMATURES: Male like adult female. Imm. female is a paler version of adult and lacks band on chest.

Voice

Song is a buzzy ascending trill, often ending with a sharp downward note, like

Undertail Pattern

Undertail coverts white; white tail spots on short tail.

"zeeeeeeeeeeee-yup." *East: Disk 3, track 10.*

Behavior and Habitat

Very active warbler that often feeds at the tips of branches. Breeds in deciduous and coniferous forests, often near water and often with Spanish moss or lichens, which are used in its nest.

May 10
May 1
Apr 20
Apr 10
Apr 1
Mar 20
Mar 10

Spring Migration

Crosses Gulf of Mexico to entire Gulf Coast; also comes from West Indies to Fla. peninsula. Migration begins early and is prolonged.

Aug 20
Sep 1
Sep 10

Fall Migration

Migrants are most commonly found along the Atlantic Coast. Winters in the West Indies, Mexico, and Cent. America.

Male

Male

Female

Fall immature
female

Tropical Parula

Parula pitiayumi   4.25"

Main Year-round Clues

- Note limited range.
- Bright yellow throat and breast with orange or golden wash across breast to belly.
- Blue-gray above with greenish patch on upper back.
- Two bold white wingbars.
- No white crescents around eyes.
- Very small, short-tailed warbler.
- Yellow on belly more extensive than in Northern Parula.

Additional Clues

MALE: Black area below and in front of eye; strong orange wash across breast.
FEMALE: No black on face; light wash across breast.
IMMATURES: Female may have no wash across breast.

Undertail Pattern

Undertail coverts white; white tail spots on short tail.

Voice

Song is a buzzy ascending trill, often ending with a sharp downward note, like "zeeeeeeeeeeee-yup." *West: Disk 4, track 26b.*

Behavior and Habitat

Very active warbler that often feeds at the tips of branches. May hold tail cocked and wings drooped. Breeds in open stands of live oak.

Spring Migration   Mar 20

Year-round resident in parts of Mexico and Cent. America. Found in open live oak woodlands with Spanish moss (used for nesting).

Fall Migration   Sep 1

Very short-distance migrant, withdrawing only from northernmost parts of range in winter.

Male

Yellow-breasted Chat

Icteria virens   7"

Main Year-round Clues

- Bright yellow throat and breast; white belly and undertail coverts.
- Olive upperparts.
- White "spectacles."
- The largest warbler.
- See also Behavior.

Additional Clues

MALE: Black lores and rich yellow underparts.
FEMALE: Dark gray lores and paler underparts.

Voice

Song an assortment of whistles, rattles, scolds, and mews given at a leisurely rate and from exposed perches or while in flight. Call is a grating "chack." *East: Disk 3, track 43.*

Undertail Pattern

White undertail coverts; long tail with no white spots.

Behavior and Habitat

Generally secretive and skulking. May fly with slow wingbeats, showing yellow underwing coverts. Breeds in dense thickets and brushy edges.

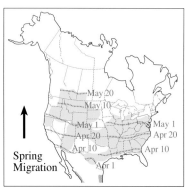

Localized as a breeder over most of the Great Plains. Eastern-breeding birds cross the Gulf of Mexico.

Winters in Mexico and Cent. America; some may winter along the East Coast as far north as Massachusetts.

Male

Yellow-rumped Warbler, "Myrtle"

Dendroica coronata   5.25"

Eastern Subspecies (Western Subspecies on p. 98)

Main Year-round Clues

(Western Subspecies on p. 98)

- Bright yellow rump. Yellow patch on sides, in front of wings.
- Streaked on breast and flanks.
- Thin white eyebrow.
- Most abundant warbler during fall migration and in winter.

Additional Clues

SPRING MALE: Yellow patch on crown, white throat, black mask. Blue-gray back.
SPRING FEMALE: Similar to male but yellow crown patch reduced, mask charcoal to brownish. Back is brownish.
FALL ADULTS AND IMMATURES: Similar to spring female but washed with more brown. Yellow on sides can be absent on imm. females (see bottom photo, p. 37).

Voice

Song a weak musical trill. Call a sharp "check." *East: Disk 3, track 16.*

Undertail Pattern

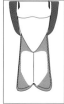

Undertail coverts white; has obvious white tail spots.

Behavior and Habitat

In winter, frequents brushy edges, especially near berries, such as bayberry and wax myrtle. In winter, often eats berries and may come to feeders for suet and fruit. Breeds in deciduous or mixed forests.

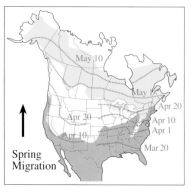

Moves north earlier and proceeds more slowly than "Audubon's." May either pass through south Tex., cross Gulf, or pass through Fla.

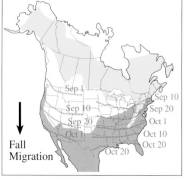

Moves south very late in fall; one of the most common and widespread fall warblers. Common in winter in much of the East.

Spring male

Spring female

Fall

Fall

Yellow-rumped Warbler, "Audubon's"

Dendroica coronata   5.25"

Western Subspecies (Eastern Subspecies on p. 96)

Main Year-round Clues

♦ Bright yellow rump. Yellow throat and yellow patch on sides, in front of wings.
♦ Streaked on breast and/or flanks.
♦ No white eyebrow.
♦ Most abundant warbler during fall migration and in winter.

Additional Clues

SPRING MALE: Yellow patch on crown and throat. Blue-gray back. Black on breast and sides.
SPRING FEMALE: Brownish gray overall with yellow crown patch reduced; yellow to pale yellow throat. Dark streaks on breast and sides.
FALL ADULTS AND IMMATURES: Similar to spring female but browner overall.

Voice

Song is a slow trill. Call is like "tchip." *West: Disk 4, track 27b.*

Undertail Pattern

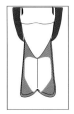

Undertail coverts white; has obvious white tail spots.

Behavior and Habitat

In winter, frequents brushy edges, especially near berries, such as bayberry and wax myrtle. In winter, often eats berries and may come to feeders for suet and fruit. Breeds in deciduous or mixed forests.

Spring Migration

Moves north later and proceeds more rapidly than "Myrtle." Breeds north to central British Columbia, east to the western Dakotas.

Fall Migration

Moves south late in fall; one of the most common and widespread fall warblers.

Spring male

Spring female

Fall

Fall

Golden-winged Warbler

Vermivora chrysoptera   4.75"

Main Year-round Clues

- Yellowish crown.
- Yellow wingbars or wing patch.
- Dark chickadee-like patch on cheek.

Additional Clues

MALE: Yellow crown, yellow wing patch, black cheek and throat.

ADULT FEMALE AND IMMATURES: Yellow crown tinged with varying amounts of green, yellow wingbars, charcoal to gray cheek and throat.

HYBRIDS: Blue-winged and Golden-winged Warblers sometimes interbreed, creating hybrids that share traits of both species. These hybrids may then breed with either species. This creates a host of variations in plumage. First-generation hybrids are usually called "Brewster's" Warbler (see p. 49), while second-generation hybrids (backcrosses) are sometimes called "Lawrence's" Warbler (shown at right).

Undertail Pattern

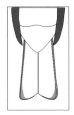

Undertail coverts white; tail with large white spots.

Voice

Song is several buzzy low-pitched notes, with the first higher than the others. Sounds like "bzeee zay zay zay." Hybrids can sing the song of either parent or a mixture of both. *East: Disk 3, track 6.*

Behavior and Habitat

Breeds in shrubby areas such as old fields, power line rights-of-way, woods openings, and brushy streamsides.

Migrates across Gulf of Mexico to Tex. and La.

Fall migration path is slightly to the east of spring path, but still across Gulf. Winters in Cent. and S. America.

Male

Male

Female

"Lawrence's"
Warbler,
hybrid

Black-throated Green Warbler

Dendroica virens   4.75"

Main Year-round Clues

- Yellow face surrounding olive ear patch.
- Green unstreaked back.
- Yellow patch on belly just behind legs.
- Streaks on flanks.

Undertail coverts white; large white tail spots.

Additional Clues

MALE: Black throat and upper breast.
FEMALE: Similar to male, but with little or no black on throat and finer streaking on the sides.
IMMATURES: Male like adult female. Female has no black on breast.

Behavior and Habitat

Eats insects and berries. Breeds in woodlands with rich understory.

Voice

Song is a series of buzzy sounds on roughly 2 pitches. Sounds much like "zee zee zee zoo zee" or "zoo zee zoozoo zee." *East: Disk 3, track 17.*

Migration is mainly across the Gulf of Mexico, but some birds also go through Fla. or around the western Gulf.

Winters in Mexico and Cent. America. Winter range may be expanding north into Tex. and Fla.

Male

Male

Female

Female

Hermit Warbler

Dendroica occidentalis   4.75"

Main Year-round Clues

- All-yellow face and forehead.
- White unstreaked belly.
- Two white wingbars.

Additional Clues

MALE: Black throat and extensive yellow crown. Gray back with variable black streaks. First-spring male has limited black on throat.

FEMALE: Throat yellowish or white with possible black mottling. Gray back with faint or no streaks.

Voice

Song is 5–6 buzzy high-pitched "zee" notes, with a change in pitch near the end. *West: Disk 4, track 29b.*

Undertail Pattern

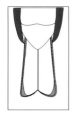

Undertail coverts white; extensive white on underside of tail.

Behavior and Habitat

Breeds in mature coniferous woods, especially with firs and pines. Feeds mostly on conifers, eating insects and spiders.

Breeds mainly in mountains, but during migration is found in desert and other lowland areas.

Winters in Cent. America. Uses narrow migration path and is rare east of Sierra Nevada and Ariz.

Male

First-spring male

Female

Golden-cheeked Warbler

Dendroica chrysoparia 4.75"

Main Year-round Clues

- Note limited range.
- All-yellow face with distinct eyeline that joins dark nape.
- Dark streaks along flanks, white belly, and usually dark throat.
- Two white wingbars.

Additional Clues

MALE: Crown and back black. Throat extensively black, and flank streaking bold.
FEMALE: Crown and back dark olive. Less extensive black on throat, and flank streaking less bold.
IMMATURES: Female in first fall may lack any black on throat.

Voice

Song is a series of buzzy sounds on roughly 2 pitches. Sounds much like "zee dee sidee zee." *East: Disk 3, track 18.*

Undertail Pattern

Undertail coverts white with a few dark streaks; large white spots on undertail.

Behavior and Habitat

Breeds in open woodlands with Ashe juniper trees. Eats insects that it gleans from leaves.

Spring Migration   Mar 10

Found only in Balcones Escarpment and Edwards Plateau of Tex.; requires oak woodlands with Ashe junipers.

Fall Migration   Jul 10

In U.S., virtually never seen away from breeding grounds. Winters in S. Cent. America, but little is known about migration.

Male

Male

Virginia's Warbler

Vermivora virginiae   *4.5"*

Main Year-round Clues

- Yellow rump and undertail coverts; pale yellow patch on breast.
- Bold white eye-ring.
- Mostly gray above and whitish below.
- See also Behavior.

Additional Clues

MALE: Chestnut crown patch, sometimes hidden; yellow patch on breast.
FEMALE: Smaller chestnut crown patch; paler yellow patch on breast.

Voice

Song is a series of 1–2 part sounds, all on same pitch or rising at end, like "sooweet sooweet sooweet sweet sweet." *West: Disk 4, track 25a.*

Undertail Pattern

Undertail coverts yellow; no white spots on gray tail.

Behavior and Habitat

Continually bobs tail up and down; generally forages low in understory. Breeds in dry woodlands, chaparral, canyons at 6,000–9,000 ft.

Spring Migration

In spring, typically seen only on breeding grounds, which are usually on brushy mountain slopes 4,000–9,000 ft. in elevation.

Fall Migration

Winters in western Mexico. Migrants pass through mountains and are uncommonly seen.

Male

Female

American Redstart, female and immature male

For main species account, see p. 118.

The American Redstart female has a gray head, olive back, and is white below. Yellow patches on sides of breast, on wings, and on either side of the base of the tail (seen when tail is spread) are distinctive for the species. The fall immature male can be identical in the field to the adult female or can be distinguished by more orange in breast patches. First-spring male may also have bits of black feathering on head and/or breast.

Female or fall immature male

Fall immature male

First-spring male

Chestnut-sided Warbler

Dendroica pensylvanica .5"

Main Year-round Clues

- Chestnut on sides of breast and/or belly (some fall birds lack this).
- Yellow or lime-green crown.
- Pale yellow wingbars.
- Whitish below.
- See also Behavior.

Additional Clues

SPRING MALE: Bright yellow crown, black eye-stripe and mustache, prominent chestnut sides; white cheek.
SPRING FEMALE: Similar, with green crown, less black on face, and less chestnut on sides.
FALL ADULTS: Lime-green crown and back. Plain gray face with bold white eyering. Chestnut on flanks is reduced.
IMMATURES: Similar to fall adults. Female usually has no chestnut on flanks. Male may have wash of chestnut on flanks.

Undertail Pattern

Undertail coverts white; large white tail spots.

Voice

Song is like "pleased, pleased, pleased to meet you." *East: Disk 3, track 12.*

Behavior and Habitat

Often holds tail cocked and wings slightly drooped. Breeds in undergrowth in cutover woods, shrubby regrowth, roadside thickets.

Winters mostly in Cent. America, also in extreme southern Mexico. Migrates across Gulf of Mexico.

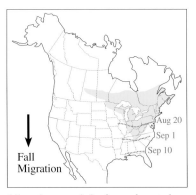

Migration route is farther to the east than in spring, with birds being more numerous on southern Atlantic Coast.

Spring male

Spring female

Fall immature male

Fall immature female

Main Year-round Clues

- Usually some trace of chestnut or buffy wash on flanks.
- Bold white wingbars.
- Dark gray legs (distinguish it from imm. Blackpoll Warbler in fall).
- Never shows streaks on breast.

Additional Clues

SPRING MALE: Distinctive chestnut crown, throat, and flanks. Bold buffy neck patch. Black "mask."
SPRING FEMALE: Similar to spring male but chestnut paler and mask grayish.
FALL ADULTS: Olive-yellow above with some streaking on back. Buffy chestnut wash along flanks.
IMMATURES: Duller than fall adults, with only a hint of buff on the flanks. Buff flanks and undertail coverts contrast with white belly.

Undertail Pattern

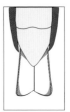

Undertail coverts buffy; extensive white tail spots.

Voice

Song is a series of high-pitched doubled notes, like "seetzy, seetzy, seetzy." *East: Disk 3, track 25.*

Behavior and Habitat

Moves about slowly and occasionally pumps tail. Breeds in coniferous forests.

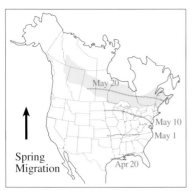

Spring Migration

May 20
May 10
May 1
Apr 20

Migrates across Gulf of Mexico. In summer, common only in Maine; uncommon to rare elsewhere. Abundance depends on spruce budworm.

Fall Migration

Aug 20
Sep 1
Sep 10
Sep 20
Oct 1

Winters in Cent. and S. America. Fall migration is more easterly, so migrants are more common along Atlantic Coast at that time.

Spring male

Spring female

Fall immature

Fall immature

Blackburnian Warbler

Dendroica fusca   4.75"

Main Year-round Clues

- Deep orange to golden yellow throat and upper breast.
- Distinctive dark triangular ear patch on orange to yellow face.
- Lower point of ear patch connects to streaking along sides of breast and on flanks.
- Conspicuous white wingbars.

Additional Clues

MALE: Throat and face deep orange in spring, orange-yellow in fall; triangular ear patch black. Extensive white on wing patch.
FEMALE: Throat and face paler orange-yellow in fall and spring; triangular cheek patch charcoal or gray. The 2 white wing-bars are separate.
IMMATURES: First-fall male similar to adult female. First-fall female paler still.

Voice

Song is a series of thin high-pitched notes, with last note very high, like "tsip

Undertail Pattern

Undertail coverts white with a possible pale yellow wash; extensive white tail spots.

tsip tsip titi tzeeeee." *East: Disk 3, track 19.*

Behavior and Habitat

Usually feeds high up in trees. Eats insects and occasionally berries. Breeds mostly in mature coniferous woods, especially with hemlocks; also sometimes in deciduous woods.

Migration is across Gulf of Mexico. Migrants usually occur in mature woodlands.

Fall migration more easterly than in spring. Winters in S. America, primarily in Andes Mountains.

Male

Male

Male

Female

American Redstart
Setophaga ruticilla   5"

Main Year-round Clues

♦ Orange or yellow patches on wings, tail, and sides of breast.
♦ White belly.
♦ See also Behavior.

Additional Clues

MALE: Black face, upperparts, and breast. Orange to orange-yellow patches on wings, tail, and sides.
FEMALE: Olive-gray face, upperparts, and breast. Yellow patches on wings, tail, and sides.
IMMATURES: Male in fall like adult female but with more orange on sides of breast. In first spring, similar but with spots of black in face, and sides may have more orange. Immature female similar to adult.

Voice

Song is a variable series of high notes, ending with a downslur. *East: Disk 3, track 29.*

Undertail Pattern

Undertail coverts with dark tips near tail; tail feathers orange (male) or yellow (female) at base, dark toward tips.

Behavior and Habitat

Frequently fans tail, exposing yellow or orange patches at base. Very active while feeding. Often takes short flights or hovers to catch insects. Breeds in deciduous and mixed woodlands, often near water.

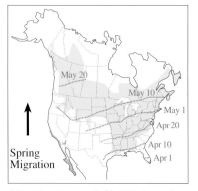

Spring Migration
May 20
May 10
May 1
Apr 20
Apr 10
Apr 1

Migration is across Gulf of Mexico and arrival is widespread along Gulf Coast. A common warbler along the entire East Coast in spring.

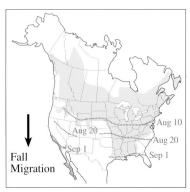

Fall Migration
Aug 10
Aug 20
Sep 1
Aug 20
Sep 1

In West, regular in small numbers during migration. Winters in Mexico and Cent. America; some also winter in south Fla., a few in Calif.

Male

Female or fall
immature
male

Fall immature
male

First-spring
male

Painted Redstart
Myioborus pictus   5.25"

Main Year-round Clues

- Note limited range.
- Large white patch on wing and white outer tail feathers.
- Red on breast and belly; black head and back.
- Thin white crescent below eye.
- See also Behavior.

Voice

Song is a low-pitched musical warble. *West: Disk 4, track 35a.*

Behavior and Habitat

Tail flicked open or held fanned. Wings may also be held out slightly, exposing white patches. Breeds in pine-oak and pinyon-juniper forests, especially in mountain canyons above 5,000 ft.

Undertail coverts barred with black and white; tail mostly white on underside.

Found year-round in pine-oak woods at elevations of 5,000–7,000 ft. Rarely seen in migration.

Some birds are only altitudinal migrants, remaining in Ariz. but moving to lower elevations in winter.

Adult

Adult

Main Year-round Clues

- Note limited range.
- Red face, throat, and upper breast.
- Black cap that extends down sides of head.
- Gray back and wings; whitish belly.
- Stubby bill, long tail.
- See also Behavior.

Undertail Pattern

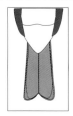

Whitish undertail coverts; gray tail with no white spots.

Additional Clues

MALE: Face bright red.
FEMALE AND IMMATURES: Face paler red.

Behavior and Habitat

Often waves its tail about. Breeds in deciduous woods along ravines, usually above 6,000 ft.

Voice

Song is a variable series of loud notes with an accented ending. *West: Disk 4, track 34b.*

Spring Migration
Apr 20

Inhabits high-altitude pine-oak woodlands or aspen groves. Found above 6,000 ft., but may be seen at lower elevations on cold spring days.

Fall Migration
Aug 20

Migrants are rarely seen, so details of migration are poorly known. Winters in Cent. America.

Male

Female

Lucy's Warbler

Vermivora luciae   4.25"

Main Year-round Clues

Undertail Pattern

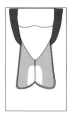

♦ Note limited range.
♦ Very small warbler that is mostly gray above and pale buffy gray below.
♦ Reddish-brown rump, white undertail coverts.
♦ Bold white eye-ring.
♦ See also Behavior.

Undertail coverts white; tail short with faint whitish spots.

Additional Clues

MALE: Chestnut cap.
FEMALE: Smaller chestnut cap often hidden.

Behavior and Habitat

Bobs tail repeatedly. Breeds in woodland and streamside areas of the arid Southwest, especially where there is mesquite. Breeds in tree holes.

Voice

Song is a rapid series of staccato notes on various pitches. *West: Disk 4, track 26a.*

Little is known about this species' migration, other than when they arrive at and depart from the breeding grounds.

Winters in western Mexico; some may also overwinter in the Rio Grande Valley along the western Tex.-Mexico border.

Male

Male

Olive Warbler

Peucedramus taeniatus   5"

Main Year-round Clues

- Note limited range.
- Yellow or orange head and upper breast.
- Variable dark mask.
- Two white wingbars, and a small white patch at the base of the primaries.
- See also Behavior.

Additional Clues

MALE: Orange head and breast; blackish mask.
FEMALE: Yellow wash on face and breast; grayish mask.
IMMATURES: Male like adult female, with some orange feathers on face. Female like adult female, but with paler yellow on breast and face.

Voice

Song is a loud "peter, peter, peter," like the song of a Tufted Titmouse. Call is a

Undertail Pattern

White undertail coverts; extensive white on underside of tail.

whistled "peuw." *West: Disk 4, track 23.*

Behavior and Habitat

Leisurely feeder; creeps along branches and feeds mostly in pines. Breeds in coniferous forests, generally above 7,000 ft.

Generally a year-round resident of high-elevation (above 7,000 ft.) conifers south through Mexico.

Northernmost breeders are very short-distance migrants, though rarely seen during migration. Others may move to lower elevation in fall.

Male

Female

Palm Warbler, breeding adult

For main species accounts, see p. 68 ("Yellow") and p. 88 ("Western").

The adult Palm Warbler in spring and summer has a chestnut crown. It also has a yellow eyebrow, dark eyeline, and dark cheek. There is also extensive yellow on the underparts of the eastern "Yellow Palm" during this time.

Spring, "Western Palm"

Spring, "Yellow Palm"

For main species account, see p. 70.

The male Cape May Warbler has a bright chestnut cheek during spring and summer and a paler chestnut cheek in fall. Note extensive yellow on underparts and face and extensive streaking on underparts. Yellow patch on sides of neck and yellow rump.

Male

Black-and-white Warbler

Mniotilta varia   5"

Main Year-round Clues

- Streaked black and white all over.
- Crown has a central white streak bordered by two black streaks.
- See also Behavior.

Additional Clues

MALE: Black ear patch and bold black streaking on white flanks.
FEMALE: Black eyeline, whitish cheek. Blurry streaking on mildly buffy flanks.
IMMATURES: First-fall male like female but no buff on flanks. First-fall female like adult female but may have more buff and paler blurry streaks on flanks.

Voice

Song is a high-pitched "weesee weesee weesee." *East: Disk 3, track 28.*

Undertail Pattern

Undertail coverts white with heavy black spotting; large white tail spots.

Behavior and Habitat

Almost always seen creeping along trunks and branches of trees, like a nuthatch, looking for insects in bark crevices. Breeds in damp deciduous and mixed woods.

Migration can be across Gulf of Mexico, through Fla., or around Gulf. More commonly than most eastern warblers, is a vagrant in the West.

Winters in Bahamas, Mexico, Cent. America, and S. America; some also winter in southern Tex. and Fla. peninsula.

Male

Male

Female

Fall immature male

Blackpoll Warbler

Dendroica striata   5.25"

Main Year-round Clues

- Large, relatively short-tailed warbler.
- Fine streaking on sides of breast and flanks.
- Yellowish or pinkish-yellow legs; yellow soles of feet.
- White wingbars.
- White undertail coverts.

Additional Clues

SPRING MALE: Distinctive black cap and white cheek.

SPRING FEMALE: Olive-gray crown and back with darker streaking. Underparts whitish or yellowish with fine streaking.

FALL ADULTS AND IMMATURES: Olive-green above. Yellowish breast and flanks variably streaked. Edges of tertials white. Strong eyeline. No buffy wash along flanks. Sides of legs can be dark brown, but backs of legs and soles of feet remain yellow. Most fall birds not reliably aged or sexed in the field.

Undertail Pattern

Undertail coverts white; white spots.

Voice

Song is a series of extremely high-pitched "seeet" notes. *East: Disk 3, track 26.*

Behavior and Habitat

A large, slow-moving warbler. Breeds in moist coniferous woods.

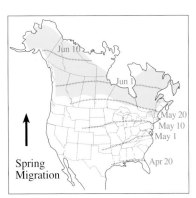

Spring Migration

Migrants cross the Gulf of Mexico; landfall is mainly in Fla. One of the latest spring migrants; common along entire East Coast.

Fall Migration

Heads east across Canada, then nonstop over ocean from northeastern U.S. to S. America. Longest migration of any N. American songbird.

Spring male

Spring female

Fall

Fall

Black-throated Gray Warbler

Dendroica nigrescens   4.75"

Main Year-round Clues

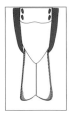

Undertail Pattern

- Distinctive head pattern with dark crown and dark mask through the eyes.
- Small yellow dot in front of the eyes.
- White belly with dark streaking along the flanks.

Undertail coverts white; extensive white on underside of tail.

Additional Clues

MALE: Head pattern black and white, throat black.
FEMALE: Head pattern dark gray and white; throat mottled with gray or clear white. Dark breastband.
IMMATURES: First-fall male similar to adult female. First-fall female has an all-white throat and breast.

Behavior and Habitat

Eats insects gleaned from leaves. Breeds in dry oak or pinyon-juniper woodland, manzanita thickets, and chaparral.

Voice

Song is a series of buzzy notes with the last note higher, like "weezy weezy weezy wheeet." *West: Disk 4, track 28a.*

Spring Migration

Migrates through most of western U.S. Typically found at lower altitudes than Townsend's and Hermit Warblers.

Fall Migration

Rare but regular vagrant along Gulf Coast in late fall; almost annual vagrant on Atlantic Coast in fall.

Male

Female

Immature female

Black-throated Blue Warbler

Dendroica caerulescens   5"

Main Year-round Clues

- Male and female look very different.
- Both have a distinctive white patch along the front edge of the wing, like a little handkerchief in a pocket.

Additional Clues

MALE: Blue-gray head and back; black face, throat, and flanks. Extensive white on upperside of outer tail feathers.
FEMALE: Brownish olive above; pale buffy below; thin pale eyebrow.
IMMATURES: Male similar to adult male. Female like adult female but slightly yellower and with smaller white patch on wing.

Voice

Song is 3–5 buzzy notes, with the last usually upslurred, like "zoo zoo zoo zeee." *East: Disk 3, track 15.*

Undertail Pattern

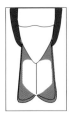

Male: Undertail coverts white; white tail spots. Female: Undertail coverts pale yellow; tail spots faint.

Behavior and Habitat

May hold wings slightly out while foraging. May come to suet feeders in fall and early winter. Breeds in mature mixed woodlands with well-developed understory, cutover areas.

May 10
May 1
Apr 20
Apr 10

Spring Migration

Migrates over Atlantic and eastern Gulf of Mexico to eastern Fla. (rare on Gulf Coast); migration then proceeds northward east of Appalachians.

Aug 20
Sep 1
Sep 10
Sep 20

Fall Migration

Main winter range is in the Bahamas and other Caribbean islands. Regular fall vagrant in the West, especially Calif.

Male

Female

Fall immature female

Cerulean Warbler

Dendroica cerulea   4.5″

Main Year-round Clues

- A small short-tailed warbler.
- Distinctive blue or turquoise upperparts.
- Streaking on flanks.
- Two conspicuous white wingbars.

Additional Clues

MALE: Cerulean blue upperparts with some black streaking on back. May have a thin whitish eyebrow in first spring. Thin breastband.

FEMALE: Turquoise to greenish upperparts, often deeper on crown. Wide yellowish eyebrow. Underparts pale yellow with faint streaking on flanks.

IMMATURES: Similar to adult female but greener above and yellower below.

Voice

Song is a 3-part series of rapid buzzy notes, beginning on one pitch, with a distinctive

Undertail Pattern

Undertail coverts white; white tail spots on relatively short tail.

fast middle section, and ending with a higher note, like "zray zray zray zazaza zreee." *East: Disk 3, track 27.*

Behavior and Habitat

Gleans or flycatches insects high in trees. Breeds in mature deciduous trees, especially near swamps and streams.

Winters in northern S. America and migrates across Gulf of Mexico; arrives in eastern Tex. and southwestern La.

Heads south via eastern Gulf Coast and Fla. Departs breeding grounds very early; migrants are infrequently seen.

Male

Male

First-spring
male

Female

Main Year-round Clues

- Brown above; uniformly yellowish, buffy, or whitish below with brown streaking.
- Bold whitish to yellowish eyebrow.
- Chin finely streaked with dots.
- Bill about the length of lores.
- Best told from similar Louisiana Waterthrush by its more compact shape (shorter bill, shorter neck, shorter legs), its tail-bobbing behavior, and its uniformly colored underparts (Louisiana Waterthrush has bicolored underparts — buff flanks and white belly).
- See also Voice, Behavior.

Undertail Pattern

Undertail coverts white, pale yellow, or buff; no tail spots.

Behavior and Habitat

Walks on the ground or at edge of shallow water while feeding. Mostly bobs just tail or rear of body (Louisiana Waterthrush bobs back half of body); tail usually moves independently of wing tips. Eats insects and mollusks. Breeds in woods with ponds or slow streams.

Voice

Song is a loud and energetic series of low-pitched notes. *East: Disk 3, track 34.*

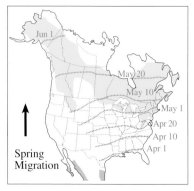

Migrates across Gulf of Mexico, as well as over ocean to Fla. Migrates later than similar Louisiana Waterthrush.

Winters in West Indies, Bahamas, Mexico, Cent. America, and S. America. As in spring, a later migrant than Louisiana Waterthrush.

Main Year-round Clues

♦ Brown above; below, bright white breast and belly contrast with pinkish-buff flanks and undertail coverts.
♦ Well-defined brown streaking below.
♦ Bold white eyebrow.
♦ Chin white and unstreaked.
♦ Bill longer than lores.
♦ Best told from similar Northern Waterthrush by its more attenuated shape (longer bill, neck, and legs), its body-bobbing behavior, and its bicolored underparts (Northern Waterthrush has uniformly colored white, buffy, or yellowish underparts).
♦ See also Voice, Behavior.

Voice

Song is 3–4 downslurred notes followed by a warbling twitter, like "louise, louise,

Undertail Pattern

White or pinkish-buff undertail coverts; brown tail with no white spots.

louise, louisianawaterthrush."
East: Disk 3, track 35.

Behavior and Habitat

Continually bobs back half of body (not just tail); tail and wing tips move together in a circular or up-down motion. Usually on ground at edge of shallow water. Breeds in wooded ravines near mountain streams.

Crosses Gulf of Mexico and arrives along most of Gulf Coast. In both directions, migrates earlier than similar Northern Waterthrush.

Winters in Mexico and Cent. America, and in West Indies. Has earliest fall migration of any warbler.

Ovenbird

Seiurus aurocapillus   5.75"

Main Year-round Clues

- Olive back, white underparts heavily streaked with black spots.
- Orange crown bordered by 2 dark brown stripes; white eye-ring on brown face.
- See also Behavior.

Voice

Song is a ringing series of 2-part notes that get louder, like "teacher, teacher, TEACHer, TEACHER." *East: Disk 3, track 33.*

Behavior and Habitat

Walks on ground when feeding, often bobbing rear up and down. Breeds in mature deciduous or mixed forests. Most often seen walking on ground or along fallen logs.

Undertail Pattern

White undertail coverts; no spots on tail.

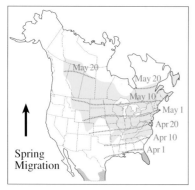

↑ Spring Migration

Migration is across Gulf of Mexico, including through Fla., or along east coast of Mexico. Found in woodlands with extensive leaf litter.

↓ Fall Migration

Winters mainly in Mexico, Cent. America, and West Indies. Winters regularly in S. Fla.

Tennessee Warbler

Vermivora peregrina   4.75"

Main Year-round Clues

♦ Dark eyeline and light eyebrow.
♦ Green back.
♦ White undertail coverts and short tail.

Additional Clues

SPRING MALE: Greenish back and gray crown, white underparts. White eyebrow.
SPRING FEMALE: Olive-gray crown. Eyebrow, throat, and breast lightly washed with yellow.
FALL ADULTS: Similar to spring adults but may be more olive-green above. Female may have some pale yellow on breast.
IMMATURES: Yellow-green above; yellow on breast and sometimes belly as well. Eyebrow yellow. Undertail can be tinged with yellow. May have faint thin yellow wingbars. Many fall adult females and immatures not reliably distinguished in the field.

Undertail Pattern

Adult undertail coverts white; tail short with small white tail spots in the male. No tail spots on female.

Voice

Song is 2–3 phrases of loud repeated notes, the last phrase fastest. Sounds like "tsit tsit tsit, tsut tsut tsut tsut, teeteeteeteetee." *East: Disk 3, track 7.*

Behavior and Habitat

Active feeder, rapidly flits about while gleaning for insects. Breeds in woods with brushy understory.

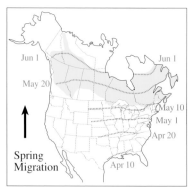

Migrates across Gulf; uncommon east of Appalachians. Forages in tall trees. Abundant in years of high spruce budworm populations.

More common on East Coast in fall than spring. Found in lower, brushier habitat than in spring.

Spring male

Spring female

Fall adult
female or
immature

Fall adult
female or
immature

Orange-crowned Warbler, Eastern

Vermivora celata   5"

Eastern Subspecies (Western Subspecies on p. 44)

Main Year-round Clues

Undertail Pattern

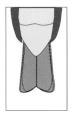

Undertail coverts yellow; no spots on grayish tail.

- Drab warbler with a lack of distinctive field marks.
- Pale yellow to olive underparts; dull olive upperparts.
- Yellow undertail coverts.
- Indistinct streaking on breast.
- Split eye-ring yellowish.

Additional Clues

IMMATURES: Imm. females are mostly gray below, with just a hint of yellow on the breast, but they still have their yellow undertail coverts. Split eye-ring whitish. Their lack of distinctiveness is in itself a clue to their identity.

Voice

Song is a high-pitched trill that trails off at the end. *East: Disk 3, track 8.*

Behavior and Habitat

When foraging, moves more slowly than most warblers. Feeds mostly low in under-brush, weedy fields, and under-story. May come to suet, seed, or hummingbird feeders in winter. Breeds in dense thick-ets, forest edges, brushy fields.

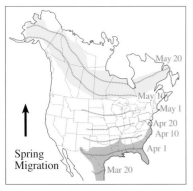

Eastern subspecies uncommon along East Coast in spring.

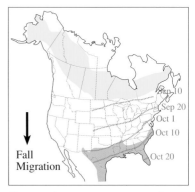

Eastern migrants more numerous along the East Coast than in spring, but still uncommon. Eastern subspecies is also a late fall migrant.

Adult

Adult

Immature

Main Year-round Clues

- Warm buffy head and breast; strong black lines on crown and through eyes.
- Olive-green back.
- See also Behavior.

Voice

Song is a dry trill on one pitch, with a mechanical sewing-machine-like quality. *East: Disk 3, track 31.*

Behavior and Habitat

Often specializes in poking into dead clusters of leaves for insects. Usually feeds in the understory, sometimes creeping along branches; when rarely on the ground, it hops. Breeds in wooded hillsides and ravines.

Undertail Pattern

Undertail coverts buffy with darker brown tips. Tail feathers dark with no white spots.

Spring Migration

May 1
Apr 20
Apr 10
Apr 1

Migrates across Gulf, and lands from Tex. to Fla. Some birds overshoot breeding range and show up in Great Lakes region.

Fall Migration

Aug 1
Aug 10

Winters in West Indies, Mexico, and Cent. America.

Swainson's Warbler
Limnothlypis swainsonii   5.25"

Main Year-round Clues

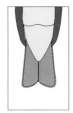

- ◆ Warm brown crown and upperparts; pale tan below.
- ◆ Pale eyebrow and brown eyeline.
- ◆ Relatively long heavy bill and short tail.
- ◆ See also Behavior.

Buffy undertail coverts; short tail with no white spots.

Voice

Song is 3–4 loud downslurred whistles followed by warbling notes that often end in a downslurred "teeu." *East: Disk 3, track 32.*

Behavior and Habitat

Usually feeds on ground, turning over leaves with its bill and quivering its rear as it walks (not hops) along. Breeds in swampy deciduous woods and, at higher elevations, along rhododendron-lined streams.

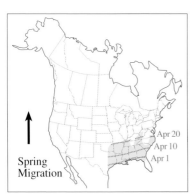

Migrates across Gulf or through Fla. Uses broad migration path, but information is lacking because migrants are so difficult to find.

Some birds head east to Bahamas via coastal Ga. and northern Fla. Winters mainly in the West Indies.

Colima Warbler

Vermivora crissalis   5.25"

Main Year-round Clues

- Note limited range.
- Brownish-gray upperparts.
- Brownish flanks; whitish belly.
- Bright golden undertail coverts; greenish-yellow rump.
- Thin white eye-ring.
- Reddish crown usually hidden.

Voice

Song is a trill, changing in pitch. *West: Disk 4, track 25b.*

Behavior and Habitat

Moves about leisurely. Feeds mostly on insects, occasionally nectar. Breeds in mountain canyons, usually above 5,500 ft.

Undertail Pattern

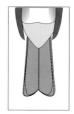

Undertail coverts golden; long tail with no spots.

Spring Migration   Apr 10

Inhabits pine-oak woods between 6,000 and 8,000 ft. Not found in U.S. outside the Chisos Mountains of Tex.

Fall Migration   July 20

Winters in western Mexico. Almost nothing is known about migration, as migrants are virtually never seen.

For main species account, see p. 136.

The Black-throated Blue Warbler female is quite different from the male, although the best way to identify it is by the distinctive white patch on the wing, also shared by the male. Otherwise, the female is grayish brown above and dull below, with a thin pale eyebrow and a dark cheek.

Adult female

Dull Fall Warblers (Immatures)

You might have heard some birders talk about how confusing it is to identify "fall warblers," and seen others throw up their hands as if to suggest there is no way to do it.

What is challenging about fall is that you have both adults and their young of that year (the immatures) migrating through. Immature male warblers most often look a lot like adult females, but immature females are usually quite a bit paler than immature males, sometimes with just a suggestion of the colors and patterns of the adults. The challenges in identification arise with a few immature females that look both very dull and quite similar.

Only a handful of these immatures are the most problematic, and we have grouped them on the next pages to help you distinguish among them. They are:

Yellow-rumped Warbler
Palm Warbler
Pine Warbler
Bay-breasted Warbler
Blackpoll Warbler
Cape May Warbler
Common Yellowthroat
Black-throated Blue Warbler

By far the most common dull species will be the immature Yellow-rumped Warbler, and we describe this species in detail at the front of the book (page 33). They are briefly touched upon here and then more attention is devoted to the immatures of the other species.

Distinguishing Immature Yellow-rumped and Palm Warblers

In fall and winter, the immature Yellow-rumped Warbler and Palm Warbler, western subspecies, are both brownish with a lot of streaking on their underparts. They can look similar, but the Palm Warbler usually bobs its tail.

Immature Yellow-rumped Warbler, "Myrtle"

For main species account, see p. 96.
Brownish overall with a streaked breast, whitish belly, and yellow rump. Head brown with a pale eyebrow and split white eye-ring. Usually has some suggestion of yellow patches just before the wing, but in some cases these are absent. Whitish undertail coverts.

Fall immature

Immature Yellow-rumped Warbler, "Audubon's"

For main species account, see p. 98.

Same as "Myrtle" but with no pale eyebrow.

Fall adult or immature

Palm Warbler, "Western Palm"

For main species account, see p. 88.

Brownish overall with a streaked breast, creamy belly, and bright yellow undertail coverts. Rump is greenish yellow. Head is brown with fine streaking on the crown; it has a bold whitish eyebrow and dark eyeline. Bobs tail continuously and often seen feeding on the ground in small flocks. Adults and immatures look similar.

Fall adult or immature

Distinguishing Immature Pine, Bay-breasted, and Blackpoll Warblers

Immature Pine, Bay-breasted, and Blackpoll Warblers are often considered to have some of the most difficult plumages to distinguish. You almost always have to use a combination of many clues, for no one clue is ever consistent or distinctive enough in all circumstances to clinch your identification. The key characteristics involve:

- Streaking on the back
- Edging of the tertials
- Leg color
- Color of the soles of the feet
- Undertail covert color and contrast with belly

If you see streaking on the back and white edges to the tertials, then you have either a Bay-breasted or Blackpoll Warbler, for Pine Warblers have neither of these. Pine Warblers also have a proportionately longer bill and tail than the other two.

Immature Pine Warbler

For main species account, see p. 50.

The Pine Warbler has an unstreaked back and dull buffy edges to its tertials. (See diagram on inside back cover.) Its undertail coverts are white, its legs are dark, and its relatively dark cheek contrasts with its lighter throat. First-fall females can be grayish overall. It is often seen in pines, may cling to tree bark, and sometimes feeds on the ground. It comes to bird feeders.

Fall immature female

Immature Bay-breasted Warbler

For main species account, see p. 114.

The easiest way to identify the Bay-breasted Warbler is to see any hint of pale chestnut along the flanks. In some immatures, this color is absent. In these cases, use the colors of the undertail coverts and the legs. The Bay-breasted has pale buffy undertail coverts and dark legs.

Fall immature

Immature Backpoll Warbler

For main species account, see p. 132.

The Blackpoll Warbler has bright white undertail coverts. Look at the legs and the soles of the feet. If the legs are dark and the soles are dark, it is probably a Bay-breasted. If the legs are pale yellow or pinkish or the soles of the feet are bright yellow, then it is a Blackpoll Warbler.

Fall

Fall

Distinguishing Immature Cape May Warbler from Immature Pine, Bay-breasted, and Blackpoll Warblers

Immature Cape May Warbler

For main species account, see p. 70.

Immature Cape May Warblers can look very dull and a little like the Pine, Blackpoll, and Bay-breasted Warblers. They are grayish overall and streaked below. Distinctive features are their greenish-yellow rump, greenish edges to their flight feathers, and yellow on the sides of their neck. Their bill is thin and slightly downcurved.

Immature

Distinguishing Immature Common Yellowthroat and Immature Black-throated Blue Warbler

These are both very plain warblers in their immature plumages, having no wingbars and no streaking.

Immature Common Yellowthroat

For main species account, see p. 82.
Look for dark brownish, unmarked upperparts and the yellow undertail coverts. The throat is sometimes pale yellow but can be brownish. Note the strong contrast between the brown cheek and the paler throat. It is a warbler of shrubby edges and often cocks its tail like a wren.

Immature female

Immature Black-throated Blue Warbler

For main species account, see p. 136.
The immature is olive-colored above and buffy below. It has a dark cheek and a thin pale eyebrow. The little "handkerchief," or white spot on the wing at the base of the primaries — so visible in adults — can be absent. Its undertail coverts are pale buffy yellow.

Immature female

Warbler Conservation Status

Here is a brief account of the conservation status of each species of warbler covered in this guide. The information is mostly a summary from the excellent series of monographs called *The Birds of North America*, published by the Philadelphia Academy of Natural Sciences, Philadelphia, Pennsylvania.

Data on population trends of North American birds are mostly derived from the records of the Breeding Bird Survey, which was started in 1966. From a biological point of view, this is a very short period of record keeping, but it is the best we have so far.

Many things can adversely influence a population of birds, including loss of breeding habitat, loss of places to get food while on migration, loss of wintering habitat, pesticide use, and bad weather, to name a few. Deciding how to weigh the relative influence of each of these factors is very difficult, and in most cases we simply do not have enough information.

The accounts are alphabetical by first name for easy reference.

American Redstart

Population trends are mixed. Decreases have occurred in the northern Maritime Provinces, northern New England, Ohio, Montana, and in general in the West. Increases have occurred in Connecticut, Wisconsin, and Quebec. American Redstarts prefer to breed in second-growth woodlands with an understory of shrubs, and this habitat can decrease as forests age or increase as forests are cut and regenerate.

Bay-breasted Warbler

This species has not shown significant changes in population over the long term. It is particularly sensitive to spruce budworm outbreaks. In eastern Canada, spruce forests are annually sprayed for budworms, and this may affect the breeding success of the Bay-breasted Warbler, which seems to depend on the budworms as a source of food during breeding.

Black-and-white Warbler

This species has been fairly stable in population as a whole, although regional populations have fluctuated during the short term. Pesticide use and forest fragmentation can negatively affect populations. In general, this is a very adaptable species, able to live in a variety of habitats.

Blackburnian Warbler

Populations are fairly stable over the long term. May be more in danger due to destruction of upland forest habitats on wintering grounds in Central and South America. One estimate suggests that a third of its winter habitat has been destroyed in the last 15 years.

Blackpoll Warbler

Long term, this species is decreasing in population, but only very slightly. The exception to this is in Newfoundland, where decreases are significant. Since this species breeds in the far North, its habitats are less likely to be influenced by human disturbances, such as logging or spraying.

Black-throated Blue Warbler

Populations are stable over the long term. On breeding ground, prefers dense shrubs with a higher tree canopy above them. Seems able to survive a variety of logging practices now being used but prefers unfragmented lands.

Black-throated Gray Warbler

Not enough is known about the populations of this species to determine trends. It is generally believed to be stable or slightly increasing. This species uses a wide variety of habitats for breeding.

Black-throated Green Warbler

Although populations can vary significantly from year to year, there is little long-term change recorded in this species. Yearly fluctuations may be due to adverse weather during breeding, such as late snowstorms in May and cold rainy weather in June. Flexibility of habitat use on its wintering grounds is much in its favor.

Blue-winged Warbler

Population is generally stable. Locally, populations can change with the availability of breeding habitat, which is primarily shrublands. These come and go as fields are abandoned and slowly evolve into shrublands and then into forests.

Canada Warbler

Overall this species is in decline, as much as 2 percent per year over the last 30 years. Declines are greatest in the Northeast. Decline may be due to the maturing of forests in the Northeast and the subsequent loss of shrub layer; also due to the loss of forested wetlands that were drained and built upon in the mid-1900s.

Cape May Warbler

Populations of this species dramatically rise and fall with the occurrence of spruce budworms in northern forests. Spraying of Canadian forests for budworms may adversely affect populations of this species in the future.

Cerulean Warbler

This species is significantly declining at an average rate of 3.7 percent per year over the last 30 years. Declines were greater in the first 15 years and less so in the last 15 years. Of major concern is loss of breeding ground habitat of mature deciduous forests along streams due to housing development and agriculture. Forest fragmentation is also a potential threat to successful breeding in this species.

Chestnut-sided Warbler

Populations have decreased steadily, although slightly, over the last 30 years. Since this species prefers to breed in early successional habitats, it can do well in areas that are regenerating from logging.

Colima Warbler

Limited breeding area in the United States is the Chisos Mountains in southwest Texas. There have been between 40 and 65 pairs of birds in this region over the last 40 years.

Common Yellowthroat

This extremely widespread species has shown only slight declines overall. Since it is a trans-Gulf migrant, it is thought that significant numbers can be lost to bad weather when the birds are making the overwater crossing.

Connecticut Warbler

There is no reliable information on population trends for this species.

Golden-cheeked Warbler

This species is limited to breeding in mature juniper-oak woodlands in central Texas. This habitat is being lost to land development, agriculture, reservoir construction,

and fragmentation. These are all causing serious declines.

Golden-winged Warbler

The range of this species is shifting north and northwestward from the Southeast, making it difficult to determine population trends. Possible reasons for declines are competition with Blue-winged Warblers, cowbird parasitism, and loss of breeding habitat.

Grace's Warbler

Not enough data to know what is happening with populations of this species. Since this species is limited to ponderosa pine for breeding, one would think that habitat degradation would be likely and a cause for declines. But not enough is known.

Hermit Warbler

There are conflicting data on the population trends of this species. Breeding Bird Survey results show stable or slightly increasing populations. And yet the breeding habitat available to this species has been drastically reduced due to logging of Douglas fir forests. It may be a case of simply not monitoring the right areas with the Breeding Bird Survey.

Hooded Warbler

Population is fairly stable overall. This species needs large unfragmented lands in which to breed. Large roads and other divisions of forests reduce available breeding habitat for this species.

Kentucky Warbler

There seem to be significant declines in population overall, but local regions can vary greatly and show increases or decreases. Sensitive to forest fragmentation.

Kirtland's Warbler

This species is a habitat specialist, preferring to live in jack pine forests that have been burned by fire about 6 years earlier. Its limited habitat in Michigan is now largely artificially managed.

Louisiana Waterthrush

In the long term, this species shows population declines in eastern states and increases in the central states. Reasons for this are unknown.

Lucy's Warbler

This species is declining throughout its range. Its preference for breeding in mesquite woods along streams and living in tree holes of mature trees is its downfall, for humans have been clearing mesquite from these areas for firewood and land development.

MacGillivray's Warbler

Populations seem to be stable overall, although there are regional variations, some with increases and others with offsetting decreases. Can benefit from the lush undergrowth that may grow in after clear-cutting, for this is where it likes to breed.

Magnolia Warbler

Populations are stable overall and increasing slightly in the Northeast. Increases in the Northeast may be a result of abandoned farms growing into young pine and deciduous tree stands where the birds like to breed.

Mourning Warbler

Populations are either stable or increasing slightly in the long term. These birds may benefit from being able to breed in the undergrowth along roads and the shrubby growth that occurs after clear-cut logging.

Nashville Warbler

Stable populations throughout range. Western populations may be increasing slightly as birds move into regeneration growth that follows clear-cuts.

Northern Parula

This species can utilize a wide variety of habitats for breeding and feeding. This undoubtedly contributes to the long-term stability of its population.

Northern Waterthrush

Populations seem stable. Wintering areas include mangroves of the Caribbean and Venezuela, which are being destroyed for firewood and papermaking. This could adversely affect our breeding populations in the future.

Olive Warbler

Within its limited range in the Southwest, there is not enough information on populations to discern trends.

Orange-crowned Warbler

Populations seem to be stable over the long term. Management practices that encourage growth of shrubs and cover add to the breeding habitat of this species.

Ovenbird

There are conflicting data on the population trends among Ovenbirds. In general, populations may be increasing in the centers of its range but decreasing at the fringes. Forest fragmentation seems to reduce breeding success in this species.

Painted Redstart

This species has a very small range in the United States, limited to the Southwest. There is not enough information to discern any population trends.

Palm Warbler

There is a significant positive trend in Palm Warbler populations in the last 30 years. Its boggy breeding habitat in the far North is rarely disturbed by humans, so far.

Pine Warbler

Overall populations have increased 1.2 percent per year over the last approximately 30 years. Even though their main breeding habitat, mature pine forests, is decreasing due to logging and land development, Pine Warblers seem able to adapt to breeding in younger stands of pine in areas of regrowth after cutting.

Prairie Warbler

In most areas, populations have decreased significantly. Reasons for the declines are not known.

Prothonotary Warbler

Populations have significantly declined over the last 30 years, more so in the Midwest than in the East. Destruction of wooded floodplains could be the problem, especially since this species needs old tree holes for nesting sites.

Red-faced Warbler

Limited range within the United States makes significant population data difficult to gather. This species is very susceptible on its breeding ground to logging of any kind, even when the logging is selective.

Swainson's Warbler

Data show a patchwork of regional declines and increases in population. This warbler is rarely common enough to gather significant data that will yield meaningful trends. Certainly its habitat of wet bottomlands along rivers is rapidly declining due to conversion to agriculture and urbanization.

Tennessee Warbler

Populations seem stable over the long term. This species can increase its populations significantly during spruce budworm outbreaks, but does not seem as dependent on the budworms as some other warblers are.

Townsend's Warbler

Population trends unclear. Better data on its presence during breeding are needed before meaningful trends can be deduced.

Tropical Parula

Limited distribution in the United States makes it impossible to discern meaningful trends.

Virginia's Warbler

Not enough data to know population trends in this species.

Wilson's Warbler

Even though in certain regions, such as the Northwest and Northeast, populations have recently risen slightly, general trends show that the population is decreasing by about 2 percent per year over the last approximately 30 years. Most likely cause for declines in western portions is the loss of streamside and riverside vegetation, which serves as breeding habitat and for food during migration.

Worm-eating Warbler

Data too sparse to yield meaningful estimates of population trends.

Yellow-breasted Chat

Data show that populations overall are stable over the last 30 years. Because it breeds in short-lived early successional habitat, population trends will vary locally.

Yellow Warbler

Population seems to be stable. This extremely widespread warbler takes advantage of even small patches of its breeding habitat — wet thickets.

Yellow-rumped Warbler

The "Myrtle" Yellow-rump has significantly increased over the last 30 years. The "Audubon's" Yellow-rump has remained stable in population. Undoubtedly, the flexibility of this species in terms of breeding habitat and foods that it will eat has helped it out.

Yellow-throated Warbler

Populations of the Yellow-throated Warbler seem to be stable. Population is expanding range to the north. On the wintering grounds it is a habitat generalist, much to its benefit.

Index to Scientific Names

Index to Common Names

Look for the bestselling
Stokes Field Guides to Birds

Each with more than 900 full-color photographs — the easiest-to-use and most comprehensive field guides to North American birds

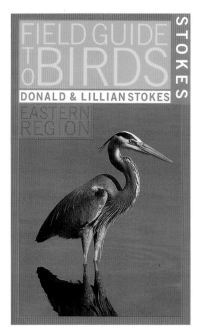 

Published by Little, Brown and Company
Available in paperback wherever books are sold

Look for the popular Stokes Backyard Nature Books

The Stokes Backyard Nature Books are large-format, illustrated guides to attracting and enjoying wildlife in your own yard — with brilliant full-color photographs throughout.

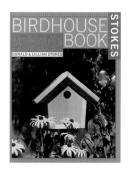

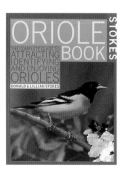

Published by Little, Brown and Company
Available in paperback wherever books are sold

Stokes Guides

Stokes Field Guides

**Stokes Field Guide to Birds:
Eastern Region**
0-316-81809-7

**Stokes Field Guide to Birds:
Western Region**
0-316-81810-0

Stokes Field Guide to Warblers
0-316-81664-7

Stokes Beginner's Guides

With full-color identification photographs —
complete information on the most common
species.

Stokes Beginner's Guide to Bats
0-316-81658-2

Stokes Beginner's Guide to Bird Feeding
0-316-81659-0

**Stokes Beginner's Guide to Birds:
Eastern Region**
0-316-81811-9

**Stokes Beginner's Guide to Birds:
Western Region**
0-316-81812-7

Stokes Beginner's Guide to Butterflies
0-316-81692-2

Stokes Beginner's Guide to Dragonflies
0-316-81679-5

Stokes Beginner's Guide to Hummingbirds
0-316-81695-7

Stokes Beginner's Guide to Shorebirds
0-316-81696-5

Stokes Backyard Nature Books

Stokes Bird Feeder Book
0-316-81733-3

Stokes Bird Gardening Book
0-316-81836-4

Stokes Birdhouse Book
0-316-81714-7

Stokes Bluebird Book
0-316-81745-7

Stokes Butterfly Book
0-316-81780-5

Stokes Hummingbird Book
0-316-81715-5

Stokes Oriole Book
0-316-81694-9

Stokes Purple Martin Book
0-316-81702-3

Stokes Wildflower Book: East of the Rockies
0-316-81786-4

Stokes Nature Guides

Uniquely informative handbooks for observing
plants and animal behavior in the wild.

Stokes Guide to Amphibians and Reptiles
0-316-81713-9

**Stokes Guide to Animal Tracking and
Behavior**
0-316-81734-1

Stokes Guide to Bird Behavior, Volume I
0-316-81725-2

Stokes Guide to Bird Behavior, Volume II
0-316-81729-5

Stokes Guide to Bird Behavior, Volume III
0-316-81717-1

Stokes Guide to Enjoying Wildflowers
0-316-81731-7

Stokes Guide to Nature in Winter
0-316-81723-6

Stokes Guide to Observing Insect Lives
0-316-81727-9

Stokes Field Guides to Bird Songs

The best sound recordings of the birds of
North America — available from Time Warner
AudioBooks

**Stokes Field Guide to Bird Songs:
Eastern Region**
3 CDs: 1-57042-483-7
3 cassettes: 1-57042-482-9

**Stokes Field Guide to Bird Songs:
Western Region**
4 CDs: 1-57042-588-4
4 cassettes: 1-57042-589-2

Published by Little, Brown and Company

Color Tab Index

Start Here by Learning Yellow-rumped Warblers

Warblers with Yellow

Extensive yellow on body

Yellow limited to throat and upper breast

Small patches of yellow

Warblers with Any Obvious Orange, Red, or Chestnut

Warblers with No Yellow, Orange, Red, or Chestnut

Black-and-white-striped

Blue or turquoise above

Brown above, boldly streaked below

Drab with few markings

Dull fall warblers (immatures)